AF867402

יֵשׁוּעַ

Aramaic Roots

The Language of God

Secrets of The Book of Enoch, Dead Sea Scrolls and The Jonathan Targum.

Bible Verses copied from BibleGateway.com and BibleHub..com

King James Version (KJV) Public Domain; Authorized (KJV)

English Standard Version (ESV) The Holy Bible, English Standard Version.
ESV® Text Edition: 2016. Copyright ©2001 by Crossway Bibles,
a publishing ministry of Good News Publishers.

New King James Version (NKJV) Scripture taken from the New King
James Version®. Copyright © 1982 by Thomas Nelson. Used by permission.
All rights reserved.

Geneva Bible, 1599 Edition. Published by Tolle Lege Press. All rights
reserved. No part of this publication may be reproduced or transmitted in
any form or by any means, electronic or mechanical, without written
permission from the publisher, except in the case of brief quotations in
articles, reviews, and broadcasts.

The Original Aramaic New Testament in Plain English- with Psalms &
Proverbs Copyright © 2007; 8th edition Copyright © 2013
All rights reserved. Used by Permission.

(See Works Cited Page 125 for references to other books, works
and quotes used in this book.)

Aramaic Roots The Language of God
Brandon Marcin and Leona Atkinson
Copyright ©2025 VII Eyes Publishing
All rights reserved. ISBN:
9798242369313

Dedication

This Book is Dedicated to Truth

"For the Son of man is come to save that **which was lost**."
Words of Jesus in Matthew 18:11 KJV

"For then will I turn to the people **a pure language**, that they may all call upon the name of the LORD, to serve him with **one consent**."
Zephaniah 3:9 KJV

"For there is nothing covered that will not be revealed,
neither hidden that will not be made known
and come into the open."
Words of Jesus in Luke 8:17
Aramaic Bible in Plain English

CHAPTER 1
Introduction to "Aramaic Roots"

Introduction to Aramaic Roots

The Aramaic Roots interpretation proposes that the original biblical worldview and linguistic structure were Aramaic, not Hebrew, and that a forgotten Pre-Mosaic Christianity treasured these Truths.

Aramaic Roots is the original, divine belief system of the Biblical Patriarchs. **Enochian Christianity** represents the earliest form of Christian thought, one rooted in the revelations of 1 Enoch and preserved in Aramaic in the Dead Sea Scrolls.

It's possible that Christianity didn't evolve from Judaism but rather preceded it as a continuation of an older, more ancient faith. Judaism places Moses as the primary lawgiver, but 1 Enoch predates Moses and presents a direct revelation from God. Judaism is an Abrahamic religion, while Aramaic Roots is the belief system of Adam, Enoch and Noah.

The Australian journal of biblical archeology states while studying the Dead Sea Scrolls: **"The Aramaic text is easily understood in comparison to its Hebrew counterpart".** We have come to the same conclusion.

Originally, we set out to make a book about the true story of Genesis. Upon further study, we found not only are the Aramaic texts more transparent but also provide additional information and context for certain scriptures. This extra information does not contradict scripture but gives us important insight into understanding it properly.

Most scholars believe the Hebrew texts came first, and the extra information in the Dead Sea Scrolls and Targum were added by later rabbinic writers. This not only lacks evidence but doesn't make logical sense. Normally, when notes are taken on a book it is shorter than the original with the longer form being the original source. We believe these Aramaic long form texts may be the original texts, with the Hebrew short form coming much later. The Aramaic texts also support a more Christian based narrative that would contradict Judaism's understanding of the Torah, showing evidence for a Christian understanding of the scripture pre-resurrection of Christ.

Introduction to Aramaic Roots

We can see in the **Talmud** that it is undoubtably commentary, and it matches Jewish Ideology. **Targum Onkelos** also matches Jewish Ideology, while the **Targum Jonathan** supports a more Christian view, along with some other books found in the Dead Sea Scrolls.

The mainstream narrative of Jewish scholars adding texts to the Dead Sea Scrolls and Jonathan Targum doesn't make sense theologically, considering the added text is never stated to be commentary nor does it reflect Jewish belief.

If Aramaic was the original language of divine communication, and the Targum Jonathan reflects oral or written traditions from Shem's line, then what we have is not commentary on scripture, but scripture before scripture. This would make the Aramaic Targums not just interpretive glosses but **possible remnants of a pre-Judaism, even pre-Flood, faith system**.

In our book, we will provide evidence for three things:

- Showing evidence for the **Aramaic Roots** of the Old and New Testament.
- Showing evidence for the ancient lost teachings of **Enochian Christianity**.
- Showing evidence that the Old Testament patriarchs believed in and followed **Yeshua (Jesus Christ)**.

We are challenging the mainstream narrative that Christian belief stems from Judaism, showing it could actually be that Judaism is basing their beliefs on something much more ancient. Could these ancient teachings have been lost? Or maybe, purposefully hidden?

Saint Augustine (354–430AD) Quote from Retractations (Retractationes), Book I, Chapter 12:
"What is now called the Christian religion existed among the ancients, and was not lacking from the beginning of the human race, until Christ Himself came in the flesh; then the **true religion, which already existed, began to be called Christian."**

Aramaic Roots Historical Evidence

Paleo-Hebrew refers to an ancient script used by the Hebrew people, primarily during the 8th century BC. It is a variant of the Phoenician alphabet, and it was used to write the Hebrew language, which is a Semitic language. Aramaic emerged earlier, around the 11th century BC as a written language. Aramaic as a spoken dialect likely existed in various forms much earlier, **this shows Aramaic was a much older language and writing style than Hebrew.**

Aramaic maintained dominance as the primary language of administration and daily life in Biblical regions for about 1,500 years, from roughly the 8th century BC to the 7th century AD. After the rise of the Neo-Assyrian and Neo-Babylonian empires, Aramaic replaced many local languages as the dominant language in the region, replacing even Hebrew in certain periods. This period will become very important later in the book.

Before Christ, in The Achaemenid Empire around the 6th–4th Century BC, **Aramaic became the official language of the Persian Empir**e, stretching from **Egypt to India**. It was used for administration, diplomacy, and trade.

After Christ, in The Roman and Sassanian Periods around the 3rd–7th Century AD. in the Roman Near East, **Aramaic was still the dominant spoken language, particularly in Syria, Palestine, and Mesopotamia**. The Sassanian Persians used Middle Persian for government but allowed Aramaic dialects (like Syriac) to thrive.

Aramaic was a far more widely spoken language than Hebrew, both in ancient times and throughout history. Aramaic was a dominant spoken language; Hebrew was a national and religious language of Jewish scholars.

Which language was more popular in 500 BC-100 AD?
10–20 million people spoke Aramaic across the Near East,
from Mesopotamia to Egypt, including Jews, Arameans, Babylonians, Assyrians, and Persians.

Aramaic Roots Historical Evidence

While roughly 100,000–500,000 **spoke Hebrew**, mostly used in religious contexts, Hebrew fell out of daily spoken use by around 200 CE. The language almost completely died, until it was revived as a spoken language in the late 19th and early 20th centuries, then becoming the official language of Israel in 1948. Aramaic continued to be spoken in various dialects until the modern era and is still spoken by some Assyrian Christian and Jewish communities today.

It would make sense if God wanted his teachings to be spread worldwide, that the scriptures would be written in the most accessible language, which would have been Aramaic not Hebrew. Based off the historical record alone, it seems more logical to assume the scriptures had Aramaic origins.

Which language is more popular today? (Modern Estimate 2024):

Aramaic Speakers: 500,000 (mostly Assyrian Christians, some Jewish groups, and isolated villages in Syria, Iraq, Iran, and Turkey).

Hebrew Speakers: 9 million (primarily in Israel, due to the 19th–20th century revival).

These figures show a possible suppression of the Aramaic language in the modern era. Could it be possible that the original language of Israel was Aramaic?

CHAPTER 2

Biblically, Who Spoke Aramaic?

Who Spoke Aramaic in the Bible?

Aram, one of the sons of Shem, is the ancestor of the Arameans, a Semitic people who lived in ancient Syria and Mesopotamia. The Aramaic language, derived from the Arameans, became one of the dominant languages of the region.

Asshur (or Ashur), one of the sons of Shem, is the ancestor of the Assyrians and the founder of the ancient Assyrian civilization who adopted Aramaic, the language of the Arameans. Aramaic was the dominant language of the region for centuries and influenced both Hebrew and Arabic.

Arpachshad (also Arphaxad), one of the sons of Shem, is particularly important because he is an ancestor of Abraham, making him a direct link in the lineage of Israel. **The descendants of Arpachshad likely contributed to the development of the Aramaic language**.

It is no secret that Abraham was "the father of many nations" (Genesis 17:4) with Christianity, Judaism & Islam, all stemming from Abrahamic belief. There is strong evidence that Abraham spoke Aramaic.

Deuteronomy 26:5 (KJV)
"And thou shalt speak and say before the LORD thy God, **A Syrian** ready to perish was my father, and he went down into Egypt, and sojourned there with a few, and became there a nation, great, mighty, and populous:"

Deuteronomy 26:5 (ESV)
"And you shall make response before the LORD your God, '**A wandering Aramean** was my father. And he went down into Egypt and sojourned there, few in number, and there he became a nation, great, mighty, and populous."

In the **Authorized King James** translation, we see Abraham is called a "Syrian". Historically in Syria, a dialect of Aramaic is the first language. In the **English Standard** translation, we see Abraham is called an "Aramean", which would be a connection to Aram (Ancient Syria). This could indicate he spoke their language which was Aramaic. It's likely he was a Aramean from Ancient Syria, based off scripture.

Who Spoke Aramaic in the Bible?

Genesis 11:31 KJV
"And Terah took Abram his son, and Lot the son of **Haran** his son's son, and Sarai his daughter in law, his son Abram's wife; and they went forth with them from **Ur of the Chaldees**, to go into the **land of Canaan**; and they came unto Haran and dwelt there."

Abraham was living in Ur of the Chaldees and later moved to Haran, **both of those regions were heavily influenced by Aramaic speaking peoples**. **Haran was in the heart of Aramean territory, where Aramaic was the dominant language.**

Traditional dating places Abraham in the early to mid-second millennium BC (around 2000–1500 BC). However, the Hebrew language as we recognize it in the biblical texts, creates a gap between the time that the stories are set and the emergence of written Hebrew.

Not only do the scriptures seem to support this claim, historically this would make sense that **if almost all the sons of Shem spoke Aramaic it would have been the language of Abraham as-well**.

Genesis Apocryphon col 19. from The Dead Sea Scrolls:
"I, Abraham……They brought gifts and requested knowledge from me. I read to them from the Book of the words of Enoch."

This shows that the teaching of 1st Enoch goes all the way back to Abraham, making it older than all the books in the Torah.

Book of Jubilees 4:21-23--speaks of Enoch:
"And he was the **first among men that are born on earth who learnt writing** and knowledge and wisdom and **who wrote down** the signs of heaven according to the order of their months in a book, that men might know the seasons of the years according to the order of their separate months.
And **he was the first to write a testimony and he testified to the sons of men among the generations of the earth**..."

Jesus Christ and the Apostles Spoke Aramaic

It is historically undisputed that Jesus' native language was Aramaic, not Hebrew or Greek. Jesus was raised in Nazareth, located in Galilee.

Jesus lived and taught in Aramaic speaking Galilee, and the common form of His name in that region was **Yeshua, which would have been his actual spoken name when he was alive**.

There is evidence that **Yeshua** originates in Aramaic. Historically, Yeshua appears in Aramaic documents centuries before the New Testament. Linguistically, Yeshua is a natural Aramaic evolution of the Hebrew Yehoshua. Culturally, **Jesus lived in an Aramaic speaking world; and He would have been called Yeshua, not Jesus**.

Aramaic Words Spoken by Jesus in the Gospels:
Matthew 27:46 KJV: "Eli, Eli, lama sabachthani? that is to say My God, my God, why hast thou forsaken me?" "Eli, Eli, lama sabachthani?" **is Aramaic, confirming it as the language Jesus spoke**.

George M. Lamas in his book a "A Key To The Original Gospels" says:
"This phrase in Aramaic means, 'My God, my God, for this I was kept. (This was my destiny-for this I was born)"'.
In Old Galilean Aramaic, "Eloi Eloi **Lema** Sabachthani" interpreted means, "Listen to my heart, this is my destiny This is why I came to earth in human form and that is to die to give you eternal life."

Mark 5:41 KJV: "And he took the damsel by the hand, and said unto her, Talitha cumi; which is, being interpreted, Damsel, I say unto thee, **arise**."
This phrase "Talitha cumi" is pure Aramaic.
Jesus spoke this when raising a young girl from the dead, some believe these words had a mystical or divine force beyond their meaning.

Mark 7:34 KJV: "And looking up to heaven, he sighed, and saith unto him, Ephphatha, that is, Be opened." This is the Aramaic imperative (Ethpathach), **showing Jesus used Aramaic in miracles**

Jesus Christ and the Apostles Spoke Aramaic

Mark 14:36 KJV: "And he said, Abba, Father, all things are possible unto thee; take away this cup from me: nevertheless, not what I will, but what thou wilt." Jesus is saying **"Abba", "Abba, Father,** "Abba" is an Aramaic word meaning "Father" and it was commonly used in ancient Christian prayers. **The phrase "Abba" is oftencited as an intimate, powerful Aramaic word that connects directly to God.**

As we see the Bible preserves multiple instances where Jesus' exact words are given in Aramaic, showing his dedicated use of the language. Although most scholars agree he could speak multiple languages, **Jesus chose to use Aramaic.**

Understanding The Biblical history of Greek, Hebrew and Aramaic:

Greek was the language the Gentiles and Pagans spoke in the time of Jesus.
Hebrew was the language of the Jewish religious elite, including the Pharisees and Sadducees in the times of Jesus.
Aramaic is the best-known language of Jesus and the Apostles.

The Gentile and Jewish Rejection of Christianity, written by Paul:
1 Corinthians 1:23 KJV: "But we preach Christ crucified, unto the **Jews a stumbling block, and unto the Greeks foolishness;"**
This verse shows us that many Jewish Elite and Gentiles rejected Christ.

Acts 24:5 ESV "For we have found this man a plague, one who stirs up riots among all the Jews throughout the world and is a **ringleader of the sect of the Nazarenes**." This verse is speaking of Paul who was preaching in Caesarea and was brought before the Roman governor Felix by the High Priest Ananias and a lawyer Tertullus for his preaching. This shows that the Nazarenes had a completely separate belief system from Judaism.

So, the question is: If Abraham and Christ spoke Aramaic, why wouldn't the Old and New Testament be translated into English from an Aramaic Source?

Jesus Christ was a Aramean

Genesis 25:20 (ESV)
"and Isaac was forty years old when he took Rebekah, the daughter of Bethuel the Aramean of Paddan-aram, the sister of Laban the **Aramean**, to be his **wife**."
Jacob was the son of Isaac and Rebekah. This verse shows all 12 tribes of Israel were at least 50% Aramean.

Luke 1:5 (KJV):
"There was in the days of Herod, the king of Judaea, a certain priest named Zacharias, of the course of Abia: and his wife was of the daughters of Aaron, and her name was Elisabeth."

This shows that Elisabeth, the cousin of Mary, mother of Jesus, was a Levite, a descendant of Aaron, the priestly line.

Luke 1:36 (KJV):
"And, behold, thy cousin Elisabeth, she hath also conceived a son in her old age…"
So, putting these together: Elisabeth is Mary's cousin, and Elisabeth is of the Levitical line (daughters of Aaron). Considering women didn't normally remarry and there is no evidence for Mary being of the tribe of Judea, off biblical texts, it's likely to assume Mary was a Levite who carried Aramean ancestry through Levi's mom, Leah.

Luke 1:27 (KJV)
"to a virgin espoused to a man whose name was Joseph, of the house of David; and the virgin's name was Mary."
Showing Jesus Christ was born of Mary, but His lineage was to be in the house of David through his earthly stepfather Joseph.

Jesus Christ was a Aramean

Luke 2:4 (KJV)
"And Joseph also went up from Galilee, out of the city of Nazareth, into Judaea, unto the city of David, which is called Bethlehem; (because he was of the house and lineage of David:)"
Joseph, described as being "of the house and lineage of David," provides Jesus with legal and tribal status through adoption, standard in Jewish law. Thus, Jesus fulfills prophecy as a son of Judah and David, even while being biologically Aramean through Mary.

Jesus Christ's birthplace was in the city of David (Bethlehem) and with his earthy father's lineage He fulfills the prophecies
in Jeremiah 23:5–6, Isaiah 11:1–2, 2 Samuel 7:12–13, and 16, and Micah 5:2.

Jesus stands at a unique intersection:
Biologically Aramean (through Mary)
Culturally Aramean (language, land and people, raised in Nazareth)
Legally Judean (through Joseph, under Jewish Law)
Prophetically Davidic (house of David; born in Bethlehem)

This union of Aramaic Roots and Judean fulfillment is no contradiction, it reflects a divine plan to unify Israel's ancestral past with its Messianic future.

One Syriac hymn (attributed to Ephrem the Syrian, 4th century) reads: "**Blessed is the Aramean tongue that was found worthy that our Lord should speak in it**."

This implies that Jesus chose the Aramean tongue, elevating it by his use.

Jesus is not just "King of the Jews" but also a Son of Aram, tying the old patriarchal world to the new covenant.

CHAPTER 3

Enoch Walked With Yeshua

Enoch Walked With Yeshua

Did Jesus Christ know the book of Enoch?

Jude 1:14-15 directly cites 1 Enoch 1:9.

"Behold, the Lord cometh with ten thousands of his saints, to execute judgment upon all,..." Jude 14-15 KJV

"And behold! He cometh with ten thousands of His holy ones
To execute judgement upon all... 1Enoch 1:9 (Charles)

This shows that 1 Enoch was recognized as authoritative by Jesus's bloodline, as The Book of Jude was written by Jesus' brother, Jude.

The oldest copies of 1 Enoch are in Aramaic, found among the Dead Sea Scrolls (4Q201–4Q212). This suggests that the book was widely read by Jesus and his disciples.

Since 1 Enoch was available in Aramaic, and Jesus's brother Jude directly quoted it, it is very possible, if not likely, that Jesus was familiar with it and supported the apostles reading it.

Does Jesus teaching line up with 1 Enoch?

Jesus frequently refers to themes found in 1 Enoch, such as the **"Son of Man"** title, which appears in 1 Enoch long before the New Testament.

Matthew 25:31 ESV: "When the Son of Man comes in his glory, and all the angels with him, then he will sit on his glorious throne."

1 Enoch 62:5 (Charles): "and pain shall seize them when they see that Son of Man sitting on the throne of his glory…"

Both talk about the **Son of Man,** sitting on a throne of glory.

John 3:13 ESV: "No one has ascended into heaven except he who descended from heaven, the Son of Man."

1 Enoch 48:2-3 (Lumpkin): "And at that hour that Son of Man was named in the presence of the Lord of Spirits, … even before the sun and the signs were created, before the stars of heaven were made..."

Both mention a divine origin of the **Son of Man.**

Enoch Walked With Yeshua

The "Epistle of Enoch" also called "The Book of Warnings and Blessings of Enoch" (chapters 91–104) provides further evidence. It contains moral exhortations and apocalyptic warnings that closely parallel Jesus' teachings in the Gospels. The blessings and woes, emphasis on the judgment of the wicked, and promises to the righteous, align with the Beatitudes and the judgment parables.

From the Aramaic Roots perspective, this suggests that Jesus and His earliest followers were not introducing a new doctrine but fulfilling and clarifying an older, Spirit-inspired tradition that had already prepared the people for the arrival of the Son of Man.

Matthew 24:37-39 KJV
"But as the days of Noah were, so shall also the coming of the Son of man be. For as in the days that were before the flood they were eating and drinking, marrying and giving in marriage, until the day that Noe entered into the ark, And knew not until the flood came, and took them all away; so shall also the coming of the Son of man be."

Jesus mentions "the days of Noah" in Matthew 24:37-39, a phrase that aligns with 1 Enoch's antediluvian narrative. We believe Christ is indirectly referencing the teachings in 1 Enoch.

If 1 Enoch was preserved in Aramaic and quoted by Jesus's own family, it shows strong evidence that early Christianity had strong Aramaic Roots in their faith by having a connection to an ancient text that would pre-date Judaism.

Words of Christ and 1 Enoch

Direct Quotes of Jesus (Yeshua) and 1 Enoch show striking similarities! The words of Enoch long pre-date the birth of Christ and the writing of the New Testament. Many of the words and teachings of Christ align with those in the ancient book of Enoch.

Matthew 5:5 KJV: "Blessed are the meek: for they shall inherit the earth."
1Enoch 5:7a,7b(Charles): "But for the elect there shall be light and joy and peace, and they shall inherit the earth."
Both mention the elect inheriting the earth

Matthew 19:28 NKJV: " So Jesus said to them, "Assuredly I say to you, that in the regeneration, when the Son of Man sits on the throne of His glory, you who have followed Me will also sit on twelve thrones, judging the twelve tribes of Israel."
1Enoch 108:12-13 (Charles): "...And I will bring forth in shining light those who have loved My holy name, and I will seat each on the throne of his honour."
Both mention seating His followers on thrones in heaven.

Matthew 26:24 NKJV: "The Son of Man indeed goes just as it is written of Him, but woe to that man by whom the Son of Man is betrayed! It would have been good for that man if he had not been born."
1Enoch 38:2 (Charles): "Where then will be the dwelling of the sinners, And where the resting-place of those who have denied the Lord of Spirits?
It had been good for them if they had not been born."
Both mention the phrase better to not be born.

Luke 6:24 NKJV: "But woe to you that are rich, for you have received your consolation."
1Enoch 94:8 (Charles): "Woe to you, ye rich, for ye have trusted in your riches, And from your riches shall ye depart,Because ye have not remembered the Most High in the days of your riches."
Both mention the phrase woe to the rich.

Words of Christ and 1 Enoch

John 5:22 NKJV: " For the Father judges no one, but has committed all judgment to the Son,"
1Enoch 69:27 (Charles): "And he sat on the throne of his glory, And the sum of judgement was given unto the Son of Man."
Both mention the Son bringing judgment.

Luke 16:26 NKJV: "...between us and you there is a great gulf fixed, so that those who want to pass from here to you cannot, nor can those from there pass to us."
1Enoch 22:9-10 (Charles): "These three have been made that the spirits of the dead might be separated. And such a division has been make (for) the spirits of the righteous, in which there is the bright spring of water."
Luke mentions the separation while Enoch expands on it.

John 14:2 NKJV: "In My Father's house are many mansions; if it were not so, I would have told you. I go to prepare a place for you."
1Enoch 45:3 (Charles): "On that day Mine Elect One shall sit on the throne of glory And shall try their works, And their places of rest shall be innumerable."
Both mention many homes in heaven.

New Testament Aligns with 1 Enoch

1 Enoch pre-dates the New Testament by centuries. Its presence among the Dead Sea Scrolls in Aramaic fragments further supports the idea that Enochian themes were deeply embedded in the apostles and shaped early messianic expectations, well before the formalization of the Greco-Roman Christian canon.

1 Enoch 48:5–6, the Elect One is described as having been concealed in the presence of God before the creation of the world. This preexistence motif directly anticipates the Christology of John 1:1–3, where the Word is with God "in the beginning" and through Him all things were made. This notion of a preexistent Messiah, so central to the Gospel of John and Paul's letters, is already fully formed in the 1 Enoch tradition, suggesting continuity, not innovation! The Gospel writers were likely drawing from a well-established tradition preserved in Ancient Aramaic.

1 Enoch 62:1–2 (Charles): "And thus the Lord commanded the kings and the mighty and the exalted, and those who dwell on the earth, and said:
'Open your eyes and lift up your horns if ye are able to recognize the Elect One.' And the Lord of Spirits seated him on the throne of His glory, And the spirit of righteousness was poured out upon him, And the word of his mouth slays all the sinners, And all the unrighteous are destroyed from before his face."
This clearly echoes Revelation 19:15, where Christ strikes the nations with the sword of His mouth. Jesus is seated on the throne of glory (Matthew 25:31), and judgment is given to Him. and when Jesus is baptized (Matthew 3:16).

1 Enoch 53:1 (Charles): "There mine eyes saw a deep valley with open mouths, and all who dwell on the earth and sea and islands shall bring to him gifts and presents and tokens of homage, but that deep valley shall not become full."
This foreshadows Psalm 72:10–11, Isaiah 60:5–7, Matthew 2:9-11, and Revelation 21:24-26 where nations bring gifts to the Messiah

New Testament Aligns with 1 Enoch

1 Enoch 61:8 (Charles): "And the Lord of Spirits placed the Elect one on the throne of glory. And he shall judge all the works of the holy above in the heaven, And in the balance shall their deeds be weighed"
This builds on the Daniel 7 vision and matches the final judgment scene in Revelation 20:11–15.

1 Enoch 62:8–9 (Charles): "And all the elect shall stand before him on that day. And all the kings and the mighty and the exalted and those who rule the earth Shall fall down before him on their faces, And worship and set their hope upon that Son of Man," This matches with Philippians 2:10–11(NKJV) that says: "that at the name of Jesus every knee should bow, of those in heaven, and of those on earth, and of those under the earth, and that every tongue should confess that Jesus Christ is Lord, to the glory of God the Father."

Enoch doesn't merely resemble the New Testament, it prefigures it. And when understood through the Aramaic Roots, it becomes clear that the Enochian texts helped shape the theological landscape into which Jesus stepped. Rather than emerging from a vacuum or purely Jewish context, early Christianity was birthed from an older Aramaic tradition rooted in Enochian prophecy, apocalyptic expectation, and a vision of divine justice already centuries in the making.

CHAPTER 4
Dead Sea Scrolls and Targum Jonathan Breakdown

Why Are the Dead Sea Scrolls Important?

The Dead Sea Scrolls are a collection of ancient biblical texts discovered between 1947 and 1956 in caves near the site of Qumran, by the Dead Sea. They date from approximately 250 BC to 68 AD and are considered one of the most significant archaeological discoveries of the 20th century.

The Dead Sea Scrolls are written in Hebrew and Aramaic, and a few texts are in Greek. They present extensive Aramaic writings that challenge the narrative that Hebrew was the original language of the scriptures.

The Dead Sea Scrolls include several Targums, which are Aramaic bibles. The fact that early Messianic communities and prophetic traditions were recorded in Aramaic shows evidence for Aramaic to be the original sacred language, predating the Hebrew centered system of Judaism. Some books appear in both Hebrew and Aramaic versions, showing it's possible that the Aramaic could be the original.

Roughly one-third of the Dead Sea Scrolls are written in Aramaic. This includes,

Book of Job was found in Hebrew and Aramaic. It is said to be one of the oldest books in the bible, and some scholars believe the Aramaic is the original.
Book of Leviticus found in Hebrew and some possible Aramaic fragments.
Book of Ezra A few parts, verses 4:8 to 6:18 and 7:12–26, were written in Aramaic.
Book of Daniel in a few parts, verses 2:4b – 7:28, are written in Aramaic.
Book of Jeremiah specifically verse 10:11 is in Aramaic.
Book of Matthew it's disputed by scholars that the book originated in Aramaic, not Hebrew.
Book of Genesis was found in Hebrew and the **Genesis Apocryphon**, which is the possible original long form version, was found only in Aramaic.
Book of Tobit was found only in Aramaic, with manuscripts in Hebrew coming much later.
Book of 1 Enoch was found only in Aramaic.

Why Are the Dead Sea Scrolls Important?

Enoch is spoken of in Jubilees 4:21-25: "And he was the first among men that are born on earth who learnt writing and knowledge and wisdom and who wrote down the signs of heaven according to the order of their months in a book, that men might know the seasons of the years according to the order of their separate months. And he was the first to write a testimony, and he testified to the sons of men among the generations of the earth, and recounted the weeks of the jubilees, and made known to them the days of the years, and set in order the months and recounted the Sabbaths of the years as we made (them) known to him. And what was and what will be he saw in a vision of his sleep, as it will happen to the children of men throughout their generations until the day of judgment; he saw and understood everything, and wrote his testimony, and placed the testimony on earth for all the children of men and for their generations."

Enoch is described as the first to learn writing, astronomy, and the heavenly order. **He is said to have written a testimony for future generation**. This shows why these Aramaic texts have been suppressed. They give us additional information that helps us understand the true story behind the Bible. Because many modern religious groups make massive amounts of money from their doctrines, the teachings of Enoch have been banned from the mainstream church.

These Aramaic traditions pre-date Rabbinic Judaism. This suggests that these ancient texts may have represented an earlier religious movement that is more similar to modern Christianity, that later Judaism sought to suppress by removing books from the Bible like 1 Enoch and shortening the texts of books like Genesis.

.

Targum Jonathan is Ancient

For those who don't have a deep knowledge of Biblical Hebrew, the **Targum Jonathan offers a more accessible translation**. Aramaic was the lingua franca of many Jews during the time the Targum was written, especially in the period after the Babylonian exile. **Many early Christians would have read the Targum not the Hebrew Torah**.

Most scholars claim the Targum Jonathan was likely written in the 100-200 AD, but the exact date is disputed. It originated in Syria, Palaestina but was adapted to Aramaic spoken in Babylonia. The Targum Jonathan could predate the Hebrew Torah. It is traditionally attributed to Jonathan ben Uzziel, a renowned Jewish scholar and disciple of the famous Rabbi Hillel, who is believed to have lived in the 1st century AD, although the contents could be much older.

Unlike Targum Onkelos, which closely follows the Masoretic Hebrew structure, Targum Jonathan is more interpretative and expansive. This suggests it could be based on an independent Aramaic tradition rather than being a mere translation of the Hebrew text.

The Bologna Torah Scroll is the oldest complete Torah scroll still in existence, dating to between 1155-1225 AD. The Leningrad Codex, which dates to around 1008–1010 AD, is the oldest complete Hebrew Bible manuscript.

We believe since there is no known author, and it is dated so early, the Targum Jonathan might be hundreds of years older than previously thought. It might not be the original but could be one of the closest full copies of the original scriptures we have to date, pre-dating the Hebrew Torah.

Most scholars argue that the Hebrew Torah came first, specifically because of its repeated reference by Rabbi Menahem Recanati 1250–1310 AD in his Perush 'Al ha-Torah. This puts the Targum Jonathan at least around the same time as the Torah Bologna Scroll.

Targum Jonathan is Ancient

Before the Babylonian exile, many scholars agree that Aramaic was widely spoken by Jews and Israelites, making it likely that early scriptural traditions existed in Aramaic before being formalized into the Hebrew canon.

The fact that Targum Jonathan differs significantly from later rabbinic Hebrew interpretations could mean it represents an independent textual lineage rather than a derivative one. The oldest portions of the Hebrew Bible (like Daniel and Ezra) already include Aramaic sections, indicating that it was a primary literary and theological language.

Mainstream Academia rejects the Targum Jonathan. It is known as a "Pseudo" book, which is another word for "Fake". Even with overwhelming evidence scholars deny logic and reason, using straw-man arguments to discredit this ancient version of the Bible. Most of the Targum Jonathan currently isn't even in English! How could this be in the modern era filled with translation technology? The only answer is because big religious groups are hiding the true Aramaic roots of the scriptures, found in the Targum Jonathan.

Targum Jonathan and 1 Enoch Connection

In 1 Enoch and Targum Jonathan, both written in Aramaic, we find the name **Azazel.** This is one of the fallen angels that contributed to the fall in Genesis 6. Both books mention this directly, showing a matching narrative between 1 Enoch and the Targum Jonathan narratives, and shows us a much older understanding of the Old Testament previously lost.

Genesis 6:4 -Targum Jonathan
"Schamchazai and **Uzziel (Azazel)**, who fell from heaven, were on the earth in those days; and also, after the sons of the Great had gone in with the daughters of men, they bare to them: and these are they who are called men who are of the world, men of names."

1 Enoch 8:1 (Charles): "And **Azazel** taught men to make swords, and knives, and shields, and breastplates, and taught them about metals of the earth and the art of working them, ..."

The Hebrew Torah also mentions the name Azazel, showing his name is backed up in canon scripture.

Leviticus 16:10 ESV (Masoretic Text) "But the goat, on which the lot fell for **Azazel,** shall be presented alive before the LORD, to be sent away for **Azazel** into the wilderness."

We learn here modern rendering they take out the mystical elements from the scriptures. We learn the original texts mentioned fallen angels by name, we learn there is not one "satan" with red horns but a multitude of god like beings that work together against humanity, Azazel being one of their chiefs.

Targum Jonathan and 1 Enoch Connection

The Masoretic Text is the best-preserved version of the Hebrew Bible, while the **Dead Sea Scrolls are older biblical writings**. Considering the Targum Jonathan's alignment with The Dead Sea Scrolls, it might have a lost ancient origin. Other Ancient Dead Sea Scroll Fragments mention Azazel as well.

Ages of Creation in the Dead Sea Scrolls 4Q180 Frag. 1 "The prophetic interpretation concerning **Azazel** and the angels who went in to the daughters of man,] [so that] they bore mighty men to them. And concerning
Azazel..."

The Dead Sea Scrolls contain Aramaic fragments that sometimes align more closely with Targumic renderings than with the Masoretic Text. Some Aramaic texts in the Qumran scrolls expand on biblical narratives similarly to the Targum Jonathan, suggesting that this was an early tradition rather than a later embellishment. The Aramaic Genesis Apocryphon from Qumran re-tells Genesis in an expanded format, resembling the way Targum Jonathan elaborates on biblical stories.

1 Enoch was also found among the Dead Sea Scrolls. Cave 4 contained over 8 copies of this ancient text. A total of at least 11 fragments were found making it one of the most copied texts among all found. This means the ancient Christians heavily relied on Enoch's writing and likely thought them to be inspired, canon accounts. This text matches heavily with the Targum Jonathan.

Targum Jonathan vs Masoretic Text

The added texts in the Targum Jonathan are necessary and align with the Dead Sea Scrolls.
Exodus 24:10 ESV Masoretic Text (MT):
"…and they saw the God of Israel. Under His feet was something like a pavement of sapphire, like the very heaven for clearness."

Exodus 24:10 Targum Jonathan:
"And Nadab and Abihu lifted up their eyes, and saw **the glory** of the God of Israel; and under the footstool of His feet which was placed **beneath His throne**, was like the work of sapphire stone... as the power of the beauty of the heavens when they are clear from clouds."

The Targum Jonathan adds reference to the throne and His glory, which matches descriptions in 1 Enoch and Daniel 7 that depict God enthroned. This aligns with ancient Aramaic and apocalyptic literature, suggesting that the Targum Jonathan preserves an early visionary tradition of God seated on a throne. It aligns with 1 Enoch, the Dead Sea Scrolls, and the Septuagint, all of which are linked to older traditions than the Masoretic Text.

Deuteronomy 32:8 KJV Masoretic Text (MT):
"When the Most High divided to the nations their inheritance, when he separated the sons of Adam, he set the bounds of the people according to the number of the **children of Israel.**"

Deuteronomy 32:8 Targum Jonathan
"...according to the number of the **seventy angels,** the chiefs of the nations."

Deuteronomy 32:8 Septuagint (LXX) and Dead Sea Scrolls (DSS):
"...according to the number of the **sons of God**."

.

Targum Jonathan vs Masoretic Text

The Targum Jonathan aligns more with the older Septuagint and Dead Sea Scrolls readings, which say sons of God rather than sons of Israel. This suggests the Targum Jonathan preserves an older tradition where divine beings governed the nations, a belief found in ancient Near Eastern and Second Temple Jewish texts. Later rabbinic texts altered this verse to remove the idea of divine beings ruling over nations, but the Targum Jonathan retains it.

These examples strongly suggest that Targum Jonathan preserves elements of an older Aramaic scriptural tradition that pre-dates the Masoretic Hebrew text.

The Jonathan Targum preserves a more mystical and supernatural tradition than the later Masoretic Text by explicitly introducing angelic beings, fallen Watchers, giants, and divine intermediaries like the Memra (Word of God) and Shekinah (Divine Presence). It expands prophetic passages with messianic and apocalyptic imagery, echoes 1 Enoch's account of angel-human unions, and frequently depicts heavenly transportation, fiery thrones, and angelic escorts similar to Enoch's visions. While the Masoretic Text presents a more restrained, literal narrative shaped by later rabbinic redaction, the Jonathan Targum preserves the older Aramaic mystical stream that bridges divine and earthly realms, aligning closely with early Christian and Enochian theology.

Many overlook the Jonathan Targum was written in Aramaic, the everyday language of Jesus Christ.

CHAPTER 5
The Patriarchs Messiah

Jesus Christ in Targum, Genesis, and Torah

Showing Jesus Christ was in Genesis based off the Aramaic texts.

Targum Jonathan Genesis 2:8
"And a garden from the Eden of the just was planted by the **Word of the Lord God,** before the creation of the world, and He made there to dwell the man when He had created him."

John 1:14 KJV - **"And the Word was made flesh, and dwelt among us"**

The Targum Jonathan says in Genesis, "the Word" is who created Eden and Man. Later in the New Testament we find in the book of John "the Word was made flesh" showing us a direct link to Yeshua (Jesus Christ) being in Genesis.

John 1:1 KJV **In the beginning was the Word, and the Word was with God, and the Word was God.**

This is not only showing us that that Jesus Christ, is in fact God. It's also showing us that **God (YahWeh) and Jesus Christ (Yeshua) are one in the same in some scriptures.**

Adam knew God. He walked and talked with God in the garden of Eden before the fall, but did he believe in God's promise of a Messiah, a Redeemer who would come?

It seems that he did, for in Genesis 3:15 after God promises a Seed that will bruise the head of the serpent, Adam names his wife Eve, which means "the mother of all living."
"And Adam called his wife's name Eve; because she was the mother of all living." Genesis 3:20 KJV

Adam believed in the hope of the coming Savior who would right the wrong that he and Eve committed, therefore Adam had faith in a coming Messiah.

Jesus Christ in Targum, Genesis, and Torah

In Exodus 12, He is the lamb of God without blemish. This matches up with 1 Enoch's "Lamb Prophecy". This matches with the New Testament in John 1:36 Jesus is called "the Lamb of God" and Revelation speaks of the Lamb also.

In Leviticus 4 the lamb without blemish is a type of Christ. Leviticus 16 Christ is represented by the high priest.

Numbers 24:17 He is the Star of Jacob. The "star" and "scepter" symbolize Jesus as the Messianic King who would come from the tribes of Israel.

This connects with the New Testament, where Jesus is described as the King of the Jews (Matthew 2:2) and the bright morning star (Revelation 22:16).

In Deuteronomy 18:18, He is the "Prophet like Moses" This is a direct prophecy of the coming Messiah, confirmed in Acts 3:22 and John 6:14.

These are only some of many accounts of Christ in the Torah, showing people had an understanding in roots of a belief of a coming Messiah, who was in fact, Jesus Christ.

Noah and Abraham Knew Christ

Did the Old Testament Patriarchs believe in a Messiah?

Noah:
"Noah was a just man, complete in good works in his generation, (and) in the fear of the Lord walked Noah." and God said to Noah: "I will establish my covenant with thee; and thou shalt go into the ark, thou, and thy sons, and thy wife, and the wives of thy sons with thee." "And they coming entered, male and female, of all flesh unto him, as the Lord had instructed him; and **the Word of the Lord** covered over the door of the ark upon the face thereof." "And the Lord spake to Noah, and to his sons with him, saying, I, behold, I establish my covenant with you, and with your children after you;"
Genesis 6:9 and 6:18, Genesis 7:16, Genesis 9:8-9 KJV

The above scriptures show that Noah and God had a close personal relationship, and that Noah believed in a coming Messiah. Plus, the Word of the Lord covered over the door of the ark. In the New Testament, the Word of the Lord is Christ. (John 1:1,14) and in John chapter 10, Jesus says "He is the Door".

Abraham:
"And God said, Sarah thy wife shall bear thee a son indeed; and thou shalt call his name Isaac: and I will establish my covenant with him for an everlasting covenant, and with his seed after him." Genesis 17:19 KJV. Targum Jonathan 17:10-11 the Lord says the covenant is "between My Word and you".

"Now to Abraham and his seed were the promises made. He saith not, And to seeds, as of many; but as of one, And to thy seed, which is Christ." Galatians 3:16 KJV. And so, Abraham looked forward to Christ, to the promised Seed.

Also, the Genesis Apocryphon col. 19 says Abraham read from the book of Enoch which contains prophecies of Christ.

Jesus Himself said: "Your father Abraham rejoiced that he would see my day. He saw it and was glad." So the Jews said to him, "You are not yet fifty years old, and have you seen Abraham?" Jesus said to them, "Truly, truly, I say to you, before Abraham was, I am." John 8:56-58 ESV

Moses Knew Christ

Moses:

Deuteronomy18:15-19 ESV "The Lord your God will raise up for you a prophet like me fromamong you, from your brothers—it is to him you shall listen—just as you desired of the Lord your God at Horeb on the day of the assembly, when you said, 'Let me not hear again the voice of the Lord my God or see this great fire any more, lest I die.' And the Lord said to me, 'They are right in what they have spoken. I will raise up for them a prophet like you from among their brothers. And I will put my words in his mouth, and he shall speak to them all that I command him. And whoever will not listen to my words that he shall speak in my name, I myself will require it of him."
Targum Jonathan says "My Word"

This is one of the clearest messianic prophecies where Moses is speaking to the Israelites. Many Jews thought the prophet Moses was speaking of was Jesus as the apostles wrote in gospels. (Luke 7:16, 24:19, Matthew 21:11, John 6:14) Peter and Stephen both quote this prophecy in reference to Jesus (Acts 3:22-23, Acts 7:37). Philip, a devoted disciple of Jesus, exclaims to Nathanael, "We have found him, of whom Moses in the law, and the prophets, did write, Jesus of Nazareth, the son of Joseph." John 1:45 KJV

Jesus Himself, also said: " For had ye believed Moses, ye would have believed me; for he wrote of me." John 5:46 KJV

Realizing Adam to Moses had a deep understanding of Christ is crucial to understanding the Aramaic Roots of the Scriptures. Mainstream Historians claim that Christianity was nonexistent until after the resurrection of Christ. This is not true based off the scriptures themselves. Just like Christians today have faith in Christ's second coming, these Patriarchs believed in His first coming.
This chapter completely dispels the idea that Judaism is the root of the scriptures. We believe it is a man-made religious group that doesn't interpret the scripture text properly and most modern Christians agree with this concept.

The majority of Christians do have faith that Judaism's understanding came first, but now, with understanding Enochian Christianity and the Aramaic Roots of the Scriptures, we can finally show hard Biblical evidence that Christianity actually could be one of the most ancient teachings on the earth.

The Scriptures are about Christ

Luke 24:25-27 KJV
"Then he said unto them, O fools, and slow of heart to believe all that the prophets have spoken: Ought not Christ to have suffered these things, and to enter into his glory? And beginning at Moses and all the prophets, he expounded unto them in all the scriptures the things concerning himself."

Jesus was rebuking His disciples for not realizing what the scriptures taught about Him. However, he used their failure to understand as an opportunity to demonstrate that all of the Old Testament in some form or fashion was about Him coming as the promised Messiah and how He now had fulfilled all those prophecies.

In John 3:9-10 ESV Jesus is speaking with a Pharisee named Nicodemus, a ruler of the Jews. Jesus was telling him that he needed to be "born again" in order to see the Kingdom of God. But Nicodemus could not understand. "Nicodemus answered and said to Him, 'How can these things be?'
Jesus answered and said to him, 'Are you the teacher of Israel and yet you do not understand these things?'"

Jesus Faces the Sanhedrin and Pilate--Luke 22:66-71 and Luke 23:1-3 KJV
"And as soon as it was day, the elders of the people and the chief priests and the scribes came together, and led him into their council, saying, 'Art thou the Christ? tell us.' And he said unto them, 'If I tell you, ye will not believe: And if I also ask you, ye will not answer me, nor let me go. Hereafter shall the Son of man sit on the right hand of the power of God.'
Then said they all, 'Art thou then the Son of God?' And he said unto them, 'Ye say that I am.' And they said, 'What need we any further witness? for we ourselves have heard of his own mouth.'"

The Scriptures are about Christ

“"And the whole multitude of them arose, and led him unto Pilate.
And they began to accuse him, saying, 'We found this fellow perverting the nation, and forbidding to give tribute to Caesar, saying that he himself is Christ a King.'And Pilate asked him, saying, 'Art thou the King of the Jews?' And he answered him and said, 'Thou sayest it.'"

Even though Jesus told the leaders and teachers of Israel, the ones who constantly studied the scriptures and had access to written testimonies of the prophets, the truth of who He was, they would not believe Him. Was it because they really knew He was speaking the truth and they were afraid, or were these great scholars really blind to the truth and not understanding what they read and taught?

We believe many in previous generations did understand. Through the ancient Aramaic Roots many anticipated the coming of Jesus Christ, some even having Him manifest to them and speak. This shows evidence that Judaism rejecting Christ means they may have rejected the prophecies of Christ in Enoch and the Torah, long before His birth on earth. The claim of ownership by the Jewish scholars could indicate the cover up of the true Aramaic roots.

Direct quote from Dialogue with Trypho by Justin Martyr, (100–165AD)
“But if you knew, Trypho, who He is that is called at one time the Angel of great counsel, and a Man by Ezekiel, and like the Son of man by Daniel, and a Child by Isaiah, and Christ and God to be worshipped by David, and Christ and a Stone by many, and Wisdom by Solomon, and Joseph and Judah and a Star by Moses, and the East by Zechariah…”

Justin constantly insists that Christianity is older than Judaism, because Christ is eternal and the Law of Moses was temporary. Justin explicitly argues that Christianity is the older root, and Judaism (the Mosaic law) was a later, temporary dispensation.

The Angel of the Lord

There is strong theological and textual evidence, especially from early Christian and Aramaic-rooted perspectives, that the Angel of the Lord (mal'ak YHWH) in the Old Testament is a pre-incarnate appearance of Jesus Christ. This belief is rooted in the fact that this angel, speaks as God, identifies Himself as YHWH, receives worship, and performs actions that align with Christ's role in the New Testament.

Hagar (Genesis 16:7–13; 21:17–19) The Angel promises her a son (Ishmael) and speaks as God.

Abraham (Genesis 22:11–18)
The Angel stops Abraham from sacrificing Isaac. The Angel speaks in the first person as God, affirming the covenant. The Angel stops the sacrifice and swears by Himself to bless Abraham. Only God swears by Himself (Hebrews 6:13)

Jacob (Genesis 31:11–13; 32:24–30; Hosea 12:3–5)
The Angel appears in a dream and claims to be the "God of Bethel." He later wrestles with a "man," identified in Hosea as an angel and also called God.

Moses (Exodus 3:2–6; Acts 7:30–35)
The Angel appears in the burning bush. Speaks as God, identifies as "I AM." Matching up with Jesus Christ. Stephen in Acts confirms it was the Angel who appeared. Jesus later quotes this in Mark 12:26–27, affirming it's about resurrection and Himself.

Elijah (1 Kings 19:5–7; 2 Kings 1:3, 15)
The Angel of the Lord appears to Elijah when he is in despair, providing food and instructions. Later sends him with a message to King Ahaziah. Also Elijah, like Enoch, was a prophet that didn't die an earthly death but was taken by God.

Samson's Parents (Judges 13)
Manoah and his wife meet the Angel, who predicts Samson's birth. The Angel accepts worship, sacrifices, and even ascends in flame, something no regular angel ever does. When this happens, the people fear they have seen God.

Showing Biblical people met "Jesus Christ" as the "Angel of the Lord."

Lamb Prophecy in 1 Enoch

Before the Old Testament and New Testament were formed.
We had the Book of the words and blessings of Enoch.

The "Lamb Prophecy" in 1 Enoch is a powerful messianic vision that symbolically foretells the coming of Christ using the image of a lamb among animals. This occurs in the section known as the Animal Apocalypse or Book of Dreams, 1 Enoch chapters 83–90.

The Animal Apocalypse (Chapters 85–90)

In this vision, humanity and history are portrayed as a sequence of animals:
Sheep = Followers of Christ
Wolves = Gentile oppressors
Rams = Jewish Elite
Lamb = The Messiah

1 Enoch 89:34 (Lumpkin):
"And I saw in this vision until that **sheep became a man** and built a house for the Lord of the sheep, and placed all the sheep in that house."

1 Enoch 90:37–38 (Charles)
"And I saw that a white bull was born, with large horns; and all the beasts of the field and all the birds of the air feared him and made petition to him all the time. And I saw till all their generations were transformed, and they all became white bulls; and **the first among them became a lamb, andthat lamb became a great animal and had great black horns on its head;and the Lord of the sheep rejoiced over it and over all the oxen.**"

Lamb Prophecy in 1 Enoch

Messianic Meaning:

- The lamb symbolizes a righteous, humble savior figure.
- The lamb that becomes a great animal with horns represents the power and kingship of the Messiah.
- The transformation of animals into white bulls reflects purity, resurrection, or transformation of the righteous under the Messiah's reign.
- The Lord of the Sheep (Jesus Christ) is shown rejoicing, signifying divine approval of this chosen one.

This lamb is distinct from previous leaders and elevated beyond them, matching Christian interpretations of Jesus as the Lamb of God (John 1:29), who overcomes the world and redeems the faithful. This shows more evidence that Jesus Christ was known and worshiped by Old Testament prophets, before the Old Testament canon was even created!

John 1:29 KJV

"The next day John seeth Jesus coming unto him, and saith, Behold the Lamb of God, which taketh away the sin of the world."

The Ancient of Days

Ancient of days prophecy in Enoch 46:1-7(Charles):

"And there I saw One who had a head of days,And His head was white like wool, And with Him was another being whose countenance had the appearance of a man, And his face was full of graciousness, like one of the holy angels.
And I asked the angel who went with me and showed me all the hidden things, concerning that Son of Man, who he was, and whence he was, (and) why he went with the Head of Days? And he answered and said unto me:
This is the son of Man who hath righteousness, With whom dwelleth righteousness, And who revealeth all the treasures of that which is hidden, Because the Lord of Spirits hath chosen him, And whose lot hath the pre-eminence before the Lord of Sprits in uprightness for ever.
And this Son of Man whom thou hast seen Shall raise up the kings and the mighty from their seats, [And the strong from their thrones] And shall loosen the reins of the strong,And break the teeth of the sinners. [And he shall put down the kings from their thrones and kingdoms] Because they do not extol and praise Him, Nor humbly acknowledge whence the kingdom was bestowed upon them.And he shall put down the countenance of the strong, And shall fill them with shame. And darkness shall be their dwelling, And worms shall be their bed, And they shall have no hope of rising from their beds, Because they do not extol the name of the Lord of Spirits. [And raise their hands against the Most High], And tread upon the earth and dwell upon it. And all their deeds manifest unrighteousness, And their power rests upon their riches, And their faith is in the gods which they have made with their hands,
And they deny the name of the Lord of Spirits,"

These verses in 1 Enoch 46 align with scriptures in Job 21:26 and 24:20, Isaiah 14:11 and 66:24, Daniel 7:9,13,22 and Daniel 10:16, Acts 12:23, and Revelation 1:13-16.

Showing it matches with narratives in the Old and New Testament of the Bible. The writers of Job, Isaiah, Daniel, Acts and Revelation. All seem to have been inspired by Enoch's ancient writings.

CHAPTER 6
Ancient Aramaic Christianity

Ancient Aramaic Christianity

Nazarenes

Nazareth, which is located in Galilee, is were Jesus was raised.
The Nazarenes weren't just "people from Nazareth.", but were those who "guarded" the true, ancient faith, a faith going back to Adam, Enoch, and Noah. **Nazarenes did not follow the Temple priesthood. They preserved older Aramaic-rooted scriptures like 1 Enoch and Targums.**

In Aramaic and Hebrew, calling someone "Natsraya" or "Notzri" **could mean "the guarded one" or "the preserved one"**, which ties to Messianic language like Isaiah 11:1 ("a branch [netzer] from Jesse"). The root word (N-Ṣ-R) had a much deeper meaning across Aramaic, Hebrew, Greek and Arabic languages "to guard," "to preserve," "to keep".

In Arabic, much later than Aramaic, "Nasrani" (نصراني) was used for the word "Christians" because they were seen as followers of al-Naṣrani (the Nazarene, Jesus). Showing the word Nazarene means a "Christian" not a "Jew".

Nazareth was tiny in Jesus' time, **and there is almost no ancient Jewish text that mentions it before the New Testament**. It was a "no-name" place, fulfilling the prophecy that Messiah would be "despised" and "of no reputation" (Isaiah 53).

Epiphanius of Salamis, a 4th-century Church Father, offers significant insights into the Nazarenes: "The Nazarene sect was before Christ."
"All Christians were called Nazarenes once, before the disciples began to be called 'Christians' at Antioch… They were so-called followers of the apostles… they dedicate themselves to the law…"— Panarion 29
This suggests that the Nazarenes, predated Jesus' ministry, indicating roots in earlier traditions. Showing evidence for an Ancient Aramaic Christian belief system, one that embraced the Messiah.

The Nazarenes, preserved ancient texts like Enoch, reflecting a lineage of belief predating mainstream Judaism. They maintained practices and languages in Aramaic that connected them to early patriarchal traditions. They operated separately from the Temple-centric Judaism, aligning more closely with early Christian and possibly Essene beliefs.

Ancient Aramaic Christianity

Essenes and the Dead Sea Scrolls

While the Essenes are mainly known from the Dead Sea Scrolls, which include a mix of Hebrew and Aramaic texts. The fact that many of these apocalyptic and wisdom texts are in Aramaic suggests that in certain contexts, Aramaic was the favored liturgical and scholarly language. The Essenes preserved many Ancient texts like 1 Enoch and the Targums.

Some Essene communities may have preferred Aramaic, it's possible that they maintained an Aramaic canon of writings that was different than the standard Hebrew texts later canonized.

Ebionites

This early Pre-Christian group is reported to have used texts like the Gospel of the Hebrews in Aramaic or versions of the Gospel of Matthew in Aramaic. While there isn't solid evidence that they favored Aramaic over the Hebrew. their reliance on Aramaic language materials suggests a preference for a Semitic linguistic tradition that could have an ancient origin.

This group followed Jesus (Yeshua) as the Messiah, but retained the Laws of Moses. Some scholars believe they revered Enoch, given their apocalyptic views and preservation of traditions rejected by Rabbinic Judaism.

Syriac Christianity / Aramean Christianity

The Peshitta is the standard version of the Bible for Syriac-speaking Christian communities. Although it's a translation of earlier Hebrew and Greek texts, **it's regarded in these communities as the authoritative version of scripture and is entirely in Aramaic.** For many Syriac Christians, the Peshitta isn't just a translation of the Bible, **it's seen as carrying the linguistic flavor and idiomatic expressions of the Aramaic spoken by Jesus and his disciples.** Some scholars argue that its language preserves an ancient Aramaic tradition that might even reflect some original idioms lost in later translations.

Syriac Christianity would be geographically the closest sect to were Jesus Christ was actually raised in the modern day. Many Syrians claim to have Aramean ancestry.

Ancient Aramaic Christianity

The Mandaeans

A small Gnostic group, which still exists today, uses a set of scriptures written in Mandaic, a dialect of Eastern Aramaic. Their primary work, the Ginza Rabba, serves as a kind of canon for their religious tradition. **The Mandaean texts are entirely in an Aramaic language form and reflect a worldview and religious practice** that is distinct from both mainstream Judaism and Christianity. They demonstrate a successful example of a religion maintaining a comprehensive Aramaic literary tradition. These texts could have been written as early as the 1st century CE.

The Assyrians

Descendants of Asshur (another son of Shem), based around Nineveh and northern Mesopotamia. The Neo-Assyrian Empire (9th–7th c. BCE), the empire adopted Aramaic as its lingua franca. This merged the identities: Assyrians were ruling, but everyone spoke Aramaic. The Assyrian adoption of Aramaic was not an accident, it prepared them to be among the first to receive Christ in His own language.

The Assyrian Church of the East often calls itself one of the earliest Christian communities that came "before Rome, before Constantinople." Since their scriptures were in Aramaic (Peshitta), they claim to preserve the earliest expression of the gospel in the language Jesus spoke.

Historically, After the fall of the Assyrian empire, both Assyrian and Aramean populations blended together culturally through Aramaic language and eventually Christianity. Whether they call themselves Assyrian or Aramean, they are essentially the same stream: the first Aramaic Christians.

Assyrian doesn't just mean the cruel empire of old; it means a people who once oppressed Israel but later carried and preserved the Aramaic gospel.
There are 3 to 6 million Assyrians alive today, 1-2 million of them Christian.

Ancient Aramaic Christianity

The Yazidi

Yazidi theology includes a supreme God who delegates authority to seven divine beings, paralleling the Seven Archangels in 1 Enoch and the divine council seen in many Aramaic-rooted texts. Their cosmology, with recurring themes of sacred mountains, angels watching over humanity, and divine intermediaries, aligns closely with both 1 and 2 Enoch. In particular, 2 Enoch's structure of heaven and hierarchy of angelic beings reflects Yazidi ideas of celestial order. Yazidi legends of divine or ancient beings shaping the world before humanity align with the Pre-Adamic narratives in Aramaic traditions, such as the Watchers' descent in Genesis 6 (as interpreted in 1 Enoch) and the multi-stage creation sequences in 2 Enoch and Jubilees.

Yazidi and Aramaic Roots link.

There is strong evidence that Aramaic was once a sacred or liturgical language in the region where Yazidism developed. While modern Yazidis primarily speak Kurmancî Kurdish, the presence of Aramaic inscriptions in Lalish, a holy site unchanged for centuries, shows that Aramaic was likely used by the Yazidi. Although the Yazidis do not speak Aramaic today, their cosmology and angelology preserve ancient Enochian and Aramaic-rooted themes. Their belief system likely preserves a pre-Abrahamic, Near Eastern religious tradition with deep connections to the same framework that produced the Book of Enoch, Targum Jonathan, and other Aramaic texts. The discovery (or preservation) of Aramaic text in Lalish is not coincidental. It provides material evidence linking the Yazidis to the broader Aramaic-rooted spiritual tradition of the ancient Near East. Yazidism may preserve a living remnant of the same stream that produced the Enochic literature, Targumic interpretation, and early Aramaic Christianity.

Unknown or Lost Sects

In regions of Mesopotamia and the Levant, where many of the Abrahamic and the patriarchal narratives take place, it is very possible that early Semitic speakers spoke in a dialect of classical Aramaic. Some scholars speculate that, given their context, most of early Christianity spoke Aramaic. These communities might have circulated a body of texts in Aramaic that represented their scriptural heritage, even if later documents were either lost or destroyed.

Armenians:
Guardian's of Enoch

The Armenian's and Ethiopian's, kept safe Enoch's sacred words.

The story of Enoch did not vanish with the rise of Mosaic law or the formation of the Hebrew Bible. Instead, it found preservation among peoples outside the later centralized Jewish canon, particularly the Armenians and the Ethiopians. These two nations, geographically distant yet spiritually aligned, acted as divinely appointed custodians of the ancient Aramaic-rooted tradition.

The oldest complete manuscript of 1 Enoch (written in classical Armenian) comes from Armenian monasteries. Around the 12th century AD, when Western Europe **had completely forgotten about the Book of Enoch**, Armenian Monks still possessed it. In the 18th century AD, European scholars re-discovered the Book of Enoch because of Armenian manuscripts.

The Armenian Apostolic Church is the **only ancient Christian tradition that officially included 1 Enoch in its biblical canon**. Armenian monks showed a deep respect for 1 Enoch, treating it as a valid source of pre-flood, angelic, and apocalyptic knowledge. Aramaic was widely spoken in Armenian regions under the Achaemenid Empire and continued as a lingua franca into the early Christian era. Many Armenian monks had direct contact with Syriac/Aramaic-speaking Christians in Mesopotamia and Edessa, absorbing Aramaic-rooted theology.

Arameans and Armenians connection.
The names don't just sound similar they have the same meaning.

Armenia = Land of the Exalted / Highlanders.
Arameans = People of the Exalted / Highlanders.

When the Neo-Assyrian Empire conquered much of the Near East (including parts of Armenia and Aram) around 9th-7th century BC, there was some cultural blending. **Some Aramean communities settled in parts of Armenia, and some Armenians traded with Arameans. This led to cultural overlap.**

Armenians:
Guardian's of Enoch

Japheth knew Enoch's words.
According Mainstream Scholarship in Genesis, Noah's sons repopulated the Earth after the Flood. While Shem became the forefather of the Semitic peoples and Ham of the African lineages, Japheth was the father of many Indo-European nations, including those who would become the Armenians.

Our theory proposes that Japheth, having access to the teachings of Enoch through Noah, preserved an Enochian tradition. This early version may have been rooted in pre-flood writings, possibly in a form older than the Hebrew script. The mountainous regions of Armenia and Anatolia, often seen as the resting place of the Ark (Mount Ararat), became a repository of ancient knowledge. It is within this cultural cradle that traces of the Enochian story continued, eventually merging with early Post-Christ Christian influences that swept through **Armenia, the first nation to adopt Christianity as a state religion in 301 AD.**

This provides two different ways 1 Enoch, within the Armenians, could have had an ancient Aramaic origin.

1. being passed down by generations of Noah.
2. from the cultural overlap around 700-900 BC.

Many Christian historians have claimed the Armenians and Arameans are the same people group which would actually make them Semitic people not Indo-European. The attire worn by Armenian women during ceremonies actually matches the depictions of Aramean women in ancient history.

Could this group have been targeted for guarding Enoch's sacred words?

Ethiopians:
Guardians of 1 Enoch

The Ethiopian Orthodox Tewahedo Church is the only church that fully preserved 1 Enoch in its canon to the modern day.

Solomon, Sheba, and the Ethiopian Enochian Tradition.
According to Ethiopian tradition, when Solomon lay with the Queen of Sheba (Makeda), their union produced Menelik I, the first emperor of Ethiopia's Solomonic dynasty. Along with him came not only royal blood, but spiritual inheritance, particularly the apocalyptic and visionary legacy of Enoch.

It's very possible that the Ethiopian religion after Solomon, preserved an Enochian form of Christianity, rather than Judaism as it later evolved under rabbinic leadership. There is no Talmudic influence in Ethiopian doctrine. Menelik is said to have preserved the worship of YHWH, without the priesthood or rabbinic law, and formed a new covenantal kingdom in Ethiopia.

Ethiopian Christianity developed its own canon independent of the Roman and Eastern Orthodox churches. Within it, 1 Enoch (also called the Book of Henok) is considered **canonical, a sacred text believed to be authentically written by Enoch**, seventh from Adam. The Ge'ez version, preserved in the Kebra Nagast and other royal chronicles, **which is not a translation from Hebrew but appears to stem from a much older Aramaic source,** suggests that the Ethiopians may have received this text from a lineage parallel to, or even predating, the post-Exilic Jewish tradition.

Ethiopian Christianity was likely influenced by ancient Syriac missionaries and pre-Chalcedonian Aramaic speaking Christians. Some Ethiopian monks may have preserved Aramaic oral traditions or encountered later Syriac versions of 1 Enoch and other Biblical texts.

Ethiopians:
Guardians of 1 Enoch

The Dead Sea Scrolls confirm that 1 Enoch was preserved in Aramaic fragments, affirming that its earliest known form was not Hebrew. The Ethiopian version, written in Ge'ez, **appears to be translated from this older Aramaic line,** not the Greek or Latin versions that circulated in the West. This makes Ethiopia one of the only nations to preserve the complete Book of Enoch
in full, unedited form, and to **canonize it as sacred scripture**.

Ethiopian Christianity **didn't just adopt a Christian identity, it developed one independently**, and its Christology (understanding of Christ) reflects a worldview from the Aramaic Roots.

The Ethiopian Church uses the phrase "Son of Man" prominently in describing Jesus, not just as a messianic figure, but as a pre-existent heavenly being, a concept originating in 1 Enoch 46–48.

The Greek Logos doctrine (John 1:1) was interpreted by the early Church Fathers using Greek metaphysics (Plato, Stoicism). Ethiopia, however, understood the Logos in a Semitic mystical way, as the Word that appeared in visions, spoke to prophets, and was inscribed on heavenly tablets. (like in 1 Enoch, Jubilees, and Qumran writings).

Ethiopian belief held that Christ, was the Word revealed to Enoch, Moses, and the prophets. They preserved ancient Enochian, Aramaic-Rooted theology, bypassing Hellenistic and Rabbinic developments.

2 Enoch and Slavic Orthodox

Slavic Christianity

The Slavs received Christianity from Byzantium via Cyril and Methodius (9th century). These missionaries used Old Church Slavonic and had many apocryphal texts in their religious libraries, including The Slavonic Book of Enoch (2 Enoch), also called Slavonic Enoch, this is a different but related text to 1 Enoch.

Dating of 2 Enoch is uncertain, but many scholars place it between 1st century BC and 1st century AD, with translations and circulation into early medieval Slavic Christianity, showing it's possible it too had an ancient origin.

2 Enoch expands on multi-layered heavens, angelic hierarchies, and a central throne, very similar to later mystical Jewish texts. The cosmology reflects pre-Mosaic ideas possibly rooted in the original Enochian tradition. The text closely resembles 1 Enoch.

2 Enoch was copied and passed down by Slavic monks, especially in Bulgaria, Serbia, and Russia. They likely believed it was a faithful account of Enoch's revelations, written down by Enoch or at least passed down from him.
2 Enoch explicitly claims to be written by Enoch himself. The text presents itself as Enoch's firsthand account of his heavenly journey, revelations, and teachings to his sons before being taken by God.

While not formally canon, 2 Enoch was respected and preserved by Slavic Christians as sacred history or inspired tradition. It was likely seen as part of the spiritual heritage handed down from Enoch through Noah, just as the Ethiopians view 1 Enoch.

2 Enoch's origin is likely Semitic, possibly based on older Aramaic traditions. Its preservation in the Slavic world suggests a divergent Christian tradition, not corrupted by Greco-Roman or post-Talmudic Jewish redactions.

3 Enoch and Jewish Mystics

Merkabah Mystics

These are later Jewish mystics (roughly 1st–6th century AD) heavily influenced by Enochian-style visions. Their name comes from "Merkabah", the divine chariot described in Ezekiel 1.

The Merkabah read and studied Aramaic Texts. These mystics were influenced by Enochian thought, specifically 3 Enoch, echoing Aramaic Enoch texts from Qumran, especially 1 Enoch and the Book of Giants.

The earliest manuscripts of 3 Enoch (Sefer Hekhalot) are all in Rabbinic or Medieval Hebrew. Likely composed between the 3rd–6th centuries AD, although it could be from earlier written traditions.

Unlike 1 Enoch (Aramaic/Ge'ez) and 2 Enoch (Greek/Slavonic), 3 Enoch shows signs of post-Talmudic Rabbinic Hebrew, more polished and philosophical. 3 Enoch is Attributed to Rabbi Ishmael ben Elisha, a 1st–2nd century High Priest. 3 Enoch talks about Rabbi Ishmael ascending to heaven and witnesses the transformation of Enoch into the archangel Metatron.

This shows how pre-rabbinic, apocalyptic Judaism evolved into an esoteric spiritual system, preserving Aramaic-style visionary themes and angelology, of something much earlier.

Aramaic often shows up in Merkabah chants or angelic dialogues. Their use of Aramaic prayers, spells and mentions of the prophet Enoch in their texts hints that the original Aramaic Roots never died, but evolved, and was kept alive underground by Christian Monks and Mystics.

The Language of Angels

Some early Christian writers acknowledged that Jesus spoke in Aramaic, a language imbued with both every day and transcendent qualities. Church Fathers such as Jerome noted that the nuances of Aramaic contributed to the depth of Jesus' teachings, suggesting that its very sound and structure could convey divine revelation.

This idea is expressed in various forms and underpins the notion that **Aramaic possessed an inherent sacred power**.

In Syriac Christian writings, the belief that **angels communicated in Aramaic,** is reflected in several texts. This belief helped solidify the idea that Aramaic was not only the language of earthly speech but also the medium through which **heavenly entities share God's message.**

1 Corinthians 13:1 KJV says:
"Though I speak with the tongues of men and of angels"

Paul, who spoke Aramaic, Greek, and Hebrew, is showing us there is an angelic language in the scriptures. Paul most likely spoke Aramaic when teaching Jews or speaking in synagogues in Judea or Syria.

Some early Jewish writers also acknowledged the supernatural power of the Aramaic Language. In Talmudic Traditions, some Jewish traditions hold that Aramaic was one of the languages used by God or angels. The Talmud (Megillah 3a) **mentions that parts of the Torah were given in Aramaic and that certain angelic communications used Aramaic.**

The Kaddish, one of the most sacred Jewish prayers, is written in Aramaic rather than Hebrew. Some traditions say this is because it is **meant to be understood by angels and all spiritual beings**.

The Language of Angels

Portions of the **Old Testament** Daniel 2–7 and Ezra 4–7 were written in Aramaic, implying it had a sacred function. 1 Enoch also being written in Aramaic, describes angelic interactions, matching this up with the Ezra and Daniel accounts. This makes some scholars believe **Aramaic was the language used in angelic visions**.

The Our Father (Lord's Prayer) is believed to have been originally spoken in Aramaic. **Some Christian mystics believe the Aramaic version has a vibrational or mystical power that is lost in translation**.

Ancient exorcisms and magical texts, such as the Babylonian incantation bowls found in Jewish and Mesopotamian contexts, invoke divine names and angelic assistance in Aramaic, suggesting it was considered **powerful in spiritual warfare**.

The Zohar, the central work of Kabbalah, often uses language that suggests Aramaic has a special, divine quality. For example, some translations have passages similar also.
"**In the language of Aramaic the secret names of God are revealed, for it is the tongue of the angels**." Although you won't always find this exact sentence in every edition of the Zohar, many commentators and translators note that the Zohar's extensive use of Aramaic is not accidental.

The widespread use of Aramaic in divine revelations, angelic messages, and mystical prayers suggests that many ancient traditions considered it sacred, while rabbinic Judaism sometimes downplays the role of Aramaic in angelic communication. Some of early Christianity, preserved the idea that Aramaic had divine power and was understood by angels. If the Enochian traditions preserved in Aramaic are truly older than Hebrew scriptures, **this could mean that Aramaic was the original language of divine revelation.**

The Language of Creation

God speaking to Abraham to hear the "Language of Creation" then he proceeds to speak, write and study in it.

Book of Jubilees 12:31-32 "And the Lord God said: 'Open his mouth and his ears that he may hear and speak with his mouth in the language that had been revealed, because it had ceased from the mouths of all human beings from the day of the overthrow (at Babel).' And I opened his mouth and his ears and his lips, and I began to speak with him in **the language of creation**. And he took **the books of his ancestors**, and these had been **written in the language of creation**, and he **transcribed them**. From that time he began to **study them**, and I made known to him what he could not understand. He studied them during the six rainy months."

The phrase "language of creation" gives us a language with origins back to creation, possibly used by Adam himself.
This shows us Abraham had ancient books written by his ancestors. This would likely include Enoch's writings.

Some translations use the phrase "the language of the fathers" again showing a deep connection to the generations before him. **This also provides solid evidence that not only were there text written long before Abraham's time, but he himself was capable of reading and writing, and he even transcribes the texts himself.**

In some translations of Jubilees 12, they use the word "Hebrew", replacing "language of creation", which is only found in modern rending of the Ethiopic. That could reflect later Jewish or Greco-Roman Christian redaction, especially from a time when Hebrew had become idealized as the sacred language.

The Language of Creation

The original Jubilees manuscript (possibly written in Aramaic) may not have used the word "Hebrew" at all, or may have used a phrase like "language of creation." Jubilees 12:31-32 is only partially preserved in the Dead Sea Scrolls. and the **critical phrase "Language of creation" does not survive in any extant Qumran fragment** of that section. Which is very interesting to say the least.

1 Enoch 82:1(Charles): "And now, my son Methuselah, all these things I am recounting to thee and writing down for thee! and I have revealed to thee everything, and given thee books concerning all these: so preserve, my son Methuselah, the books from thy father's hand, and (see) that thou deliver them to the generations of the world."
This shows Enoch told his son to write down his teaching, so that it would be saved for future generations of mankind.

In the Genesis Apocryphon (long form of Genesis) it said that Abraham read the book of Enoch. We know that the oldest copy of Enoch was written in Aramaic. Could 1 Enoch then be one of the "books of his ancestors" in the book of Jubilees?

Targum Jonathan on Genesis 11:1 "And all the earth was (of) one language, and one speech, and one counsel. In the **holy language** spake they, **that by which the world had been created at the beginning."**

The "holy language" could be the same as the "language of creation". We know the language Abraham likely spoke was Aramaic. This could indicate the original language of creation was indeed Aramaic or a proto form of it.

CHAPTER 7
Linguistic Evidence

Linguistic Evidence

We find in the Hebrew Torah some phrases seem to have an Aramaic origin. We can find a prime example of this in the story of Jacob and Laban making a covenant, the text records two names for the same place.

Genesis 31:47 KJV
"And Laban called it Jegar-sahadutha, but Jacob called it Galeed."
This is a rare instance where the Torah itself presents an explicit Aramaic vs. Hebrew contrast.

Jegar-sahadutha" (יגר שהדותא) is Aramaic, meaning "Heap of Witness."
Galeed" (גלעד) is Hebrew, also meaning "Heap of Witness."

Laban is from Aram-Naharaim, and his speech reflects an Aramaic linguistic background. This suggests that Aramaic was the dominant language in Mesopotamian regions at the time, reinforcing the idea that early patriarchal narratives may have originally been written in Aramaic rather than Hebrew.

The Hebrew Word "Galeed" feels like a later adaptation. If Aramaic were the dominant spoken language during Jacob's time, why would the Hebrew form of the name even be necessary? Some scholars speculate that the Hebrew version was inserted later to align with the developing Israelite identity, **meaning the Aramaic name was likely the original**.

Exodus 3:14 KJV – "**I AM THAT I AM**"
The structure of this phrase is unique. Some scholars argue that this construction, which uses repetition with a linking particle (אשר), is more typical of Aramaic than standard Biblical Hebrew.

Genesis 15:13 KJV
"And he said unto Abram, Know of a surety that thy seed shall be a stranger in a land that is not theirs, and shall serve them; and they shall afflict them four hundred years;" The phrase "they will serve them, and they will afflict them" is an example of emphatic repetition, which is more characteristic of Aramaic than classical Hebrew narrative style.

Linguistic Evidence

Numbers 22:6 Peshitta
"...for I know that whomever you bless is blessed, and whomever you curse is cursed."
Relative Clauses That Resemble Aramaic Word Order: The structure of "whomever you bless is blessed" mirrors Aramaic idiomatic structure, what we see in Aramaic texts like Targums. This relative clause construction ("whomever + verb + result") is more natural in Aramaic than in classical Biblical Hebrew, which tends to structure such statements differently.

Peter's original name in Aramaic was כֵּיפָא (Kepha, ܟܐܦܐ in Syriac script), meaning "rock" or "stone."
John 1:42 KJV – Jesus renames Simon:
"...thou shalt be called Cephas" (which is translated as Peter) Here, "Cephas" is the Greek transliteration of Kepha, showing that **Peter's original name was Aramaic, not Greek**.

The Greek New Testament contains dozens of Semitic idioms and structures that don't make grammatical sense in Greek, but do in Aramaic,

"Son of man" (bar enasha) is an Aramaic idiom Jesus uses frequently, and it's word-for-word awkward in Greek.

"Blessed are the poor in spirit" (Matthew 5:3) uses a form that mirrors the Aramaic construct "tubi l…" (cf. 1 Enoch and Psalms in the Dead Sea Scrolls).

Parallelisms and poetic rhythm in many sayings of Jesus resemble Aramaic wisdom tradition more than Hebrew or Greek literature.

Aramaic is not a side language in Scripture, it shapes major texts and may even represent older or more original versions of biblical traditions, especially in Job, Daniel, and 1 Enoch.

Aramaic Words Hold Mystical Meanings

While Hebrew is known for its layered meanings and root-based wordplay, Aramaic may retain even older semantic structures, that connect more directly to spiritual realities. Its terms often carry expanded or even metaphysical meanings that Hebrew later formalized.

In Hebrew, **Ruach** Typically translated as "spirit" or "wind" used to describe the Holy Spirit, wind, breath, or emotional states.

In Aramaic, **ruḥa** is often used in early Christian texts to refer to the Holy Spirit (Ruḥa d-Qudsha). This carries not just the force of wind but also the vitalizing essence or divine presence, which connects to the invisible yet powerful, a key theme in Enochian thought and mysticism. The "a" ending in Aramaic gives it a feminine aspect (grammatically), which may hint at a softer, nurturing spiritual force, a contrast to masculine depictions in later theology.

In Hebrew, **Nephesh** refers to the soul, but also appetite, emotion, or life itself, sometimes used interchangeably with "life" or "person."

In Aramaic **napsha**, retains the life-breath meaning but also adds the sense of conscious being, essence, or identity, deeply connected with personhood, which in Aramaic thought isn't merely biological but spiritual presence. This might explain why in Job, an Aramaic-heavy book, "soul" is described not just as life-force but something that suffers, communes, and pleads before God.

In Hebrew, **Bar** is often seen only in Aramaic contexts (like Psalm 2:12) where it means "son," whereas the Hebrew equivalent is "ben."

In Aramaic, **bar,** means "son," but also "grain" and "pure." It implies both physical and spiritual lineage, a seed, a purified heir. Jesus' use of bar nasha (Son of Man) taps into this layered meaning.

In Hebrew, the equivalent is **ben**, which simply means son in a genealogical sense. The deeper symbolism is dropped in Greek, which gives us **huios**, again just a term of kinship or legal heirship—no sense of purity or archetype.

Aramaic Words Hold Mystical Meanings

In Aramaic, **Shlama**, is a word often translated as "peace," but it goes beyond the absence of conflict. It means wholeness, harmony, restoration and spiritual alignment between heaven and earth.

In Hebrew, **shalom** retains much of this, but it can also refer to political or social peace.
In Greek, the word **eirēnē** becomes even more external, typically meaning peace in terms of calm or truce—losing the internal, spiritual wholeness that the Aramaic word **shlama** conveys.

In these examples, we see a pattern, Aramaic root words often begin as living, relational, and mystical terms, while Hebrew systematizes them, and Greek eventually abstracts them into categories of thought or doctrine. The further you move away from Aramaic, the more you lose the language's original meaning.

Targum Jonathan, unlike Targum Onkelos (which is more literal), includes expansive interpretations, mythic elements, and angelology. This suggests it may derive from older traditions rather than simply reacting to the Masoretic Hebrew.

Targum Jonathan's vivid narratives and references to spirits, giants, and divine judgment parallel 1 Enoch written in Aramaic. Were both these texts drawing from the same ancient tradition preserved by Noah's righteous lineage?

The Geneva Bible Footnotes Used Targum Jonathan

The Geneva Bible (1560) is one of the earliest English Protestant translations of the Bible, predating the King James Version by over 50 years. It was the first English Bible with extensive marginal notes, drawn from Reformation-era theology, Hebrew traditions, and occasionally Aramaic commentaries, **including the Targum Jonathan**.

Isaiah 9:6 Geneva Bible:(GNV) "For unto us a child is born, and unto us a Son is given: and the government is upon his shoulder, and he shall call his name, Wonderful, Counselor, The mighty God, The everlasting Father, The prince of peace."

In the Marginal Notes, they occasionally cite interpretations found in the Targum Onkelos or Targum Jonathan. This specific verse identifies the child as "the Messiah" and elaborates with a cosmic role in judgment and governance. This agreement suggests translators drew on Aramaic-messianic tradition, affirming that Aramaic texts preserved Ancient Christian theology.

Daniel 7:13 – **"The Son of Man"**
Geneva Bible Text:(GNV)
"As I beheld in visions by night, behold, one like the son of man came in the clouds of heaven, and approached unto the Ancient of days, and they brought him before him."
Geneva Marginal Note: "(a) By this is meant the kingdom of Christ, which was given to him by his Father."
Targum Jonathan Interpretation: Identifies the "Son of Man" as the Messiah, who will establish an everlasting kingdom.

The Geneva Bible and Targum Jonathan interpretations both recognize the "Son of Man" as a messianic figure, aligning with early Christian theology regarding Christ's divine authority and eternal kingdom. The term "Son of man" appears in 1 Enoch, before the New Testament was written.

The Geneva Bible Footnotes Used Targum Jonathan

In prophetic books like **Daniel, Isaiah,** and **Ezekiel**, the Geneva Bible's annotations reference:
"Angels set over kingdoms"
"Stars as symbolic of rulers"
"The Ancient of Days" and "Son of Man" as divine figures.

These are core motifs in Targum Jonathan and 1 Enoch, angelic watchers, divine thrones, and cosmic justice. The Geneva Bible uses these in a literal-spiritual way, preserving the Aramaic view of the scriptures.

The Genva bible interprets Genesis 6:2 "sons of God" as angelic beings, in agreement with Targum Jonathan, 1 Enoch, and the Book of Jubilees. Instead of the later Rabbinic reinterpretation (that they were human rulers).

The Geneva Bible indirectly supports the Aramaic roots by:
drawing messianic theology from traditions that align with the Targum Jonathan and the Dead Sea Scrolls and preserves angelology and apocalyptic themes common in Aramaic Enochian literature. It translates key texts in ways that harmonize with the Targum Jonathan's interpretive layers, especially on prophecy and spiritual hierarch.

The Aramaic language is not merely a footnote in biblical history, it is a thread that runs through the prophets, the apostles, and even the very words of Christ. The presence of Aramaic in Scripture is not incidental. It reveals a deeper linguistic root system, one that may predate and underpin the Hebrew texts we know today.

The NKJV References Targum And The Dead Sea Scrolls.

The New King James Version (NKJV) is largely based on the Masoretic Hebrew Text, however, the NKJV includes footnotes that reference alternative ancient sources such as the Targum, Septuagint (LXX), Dead Sea Scrolls, and Vulgate. These footnotes offer crucial insight into older traditions of biblical texts. **This validates that Aramaic texts were recognized, not dismissed by modern Bible translators**.

The New King James (NKJV) footnotes provide a breadcrumb trail for modern readers to trace older linguistic and theological ideas. These include the Aramaic voice of early believers, likely closer to Enochian Christianity, which predates and stands apart from both Rabbinic Judaism and Greco-Roman theology.

One such example appears in Isaiah 49:17, where the NKJV footnote acknowledges that the Targum, Dead Sea Scrolls, Septuagint, and Vulgate all use the word "builders" instead of "sons", pointing to an interpretive tradition more aligned with Aramaic thought and idiom.

The NKJV footnotes occasionally reference the Targum throughout the Prophets, especially in texts like:

Isaiah 9:6 – The Messianic title "Mighty God" is elaborated in the Targum as referring to the Messiah, not just to God the Father.

Isaiah 53 – The Targum explicitly names the Servant as the Messiah, while the Masoretic Hebrew leaves it ambiguous. The NKJV doesn't always note this, but modern study Bibles do.

These differences show that Aramaic tradition interpreted messianic prophecy more overtly, suggesting that the Targum preserved a pre-rabbinic understanding of the Messiah.

The NKJV References Targum And The Dead Sea Scrolls.

The New Kings James (NKJV) affirms the authority of the Targum by including it among sources like the Septuagint and Dead Sea Scrolls.

This shows that the Targum was not merely commentary but was seen as a **textual witness of legitimate variant readings**.

There are many other English translations influenced by Targum Jonathan. Justin Martyr, Origen, and Tertullian often quote Old Testament prophecies in ways that match Targum Jonathan, particularly regarding the Messiah's suffering, divine nature, and cosmic reign.

Here are a few Bible versions that either draw on the Targum directly, consult it for interpretation, or have similar narratives.

- NET Bible, extensive footnotes cite Targum Jonathan for prophetic passag es.
- ESV and NRSV w/ Apocrypha, used Targum Jonathan in footnotes for interpretive clarity.
- The Aramaic Bible: Targums series, academic English translation of the Targum Jonathan directly.
- The Peshitta, like the Targum, is in Aramaic and often agrees with Targum Jonathan in the Prophets.
- The Ethiopian Bible: Preserves texts like 1 Enoch and often aligns with Targum Jonathan.

Aramaic Roots Scholarly Support

These scholars collectively support the perspective that Aramaic played a foundational role in the development of Hebrew. Some even suggesting Hebrew was made to oppose the Aramaic.

George Lamsa

An Aramaic speaking renowned Assyrian biblical scholar. He asserted that the New Testament was originally written in Aramaic, not Greek. Lamsa translated the Bible from the Aramaic Peshitta in 1933 and argued that Aramaic is the original language of scripture and spiritual truth.
Notable Quote of Lamsa: "**The Gospels, as well as the Epistles, were written in Aramaic, the language of the Jewish people in Palestine and in the Greco-Roman world.**"

Dr. Rocco Errico

An American minister and biblical scholar. He is the founder of the Noohra Foundation, an organization dedicated to Aramaic biblical research, which indirectly supports the "Aramaic Roots" for the New Testament and spiritual teachings. **He advocates for interpreting Jesus's teachings within their original Aramaic linguistic and cultural framework**.

Edward Horowitz

A Jewish-American linguist and author of "How the Hebrew Language Grew". Horowitz explores the development of Hebrew and suggests that **Hebrew evolved by adapting and modifying elements from Aramaic**.

Israel Knohl

An Israeli biblical scholar specializing in the Dead Sea Scrolls. His work indicates that Aramaic was often the language of spiritual and prophetic writings, while Hebrew was reserved for formal religious practices.
Some of his work on early messianic expectations in Second Temple Judaism hints at the possibility that **Hebrew was standardized in opposition to more mystical, Aramaic speaking sects.**

Aramaic Roots Scholarly Support

Paul Kahle

A German orientalist and biblical scholar known for his work on the Masoretic Text and Targums. Kahle argued that the Aramaic Targums might preserve older biblical readings than the standardized Hebrew texts.

He suggested that the Hebrew Bible underwent a process of standardization that **may have suppressed earlier Aramaic traditions** and noted that **Targums may preserve ancient teachings.**

Louis Cappel

A French Protestant scholar, Cappel critically examined the Hebrew Masoretic Text. He proposed that the square Hebrew script was adopted from Aramaic during the Babylonian exile, suggesting that earlier versions of the texts, might have been Aramaic scripts. Cappel's analysis indicated that some Old Testament vowel points and accents in **Hebrew were later additions, potentially derived from Aramaic traditions**.

R.H. Charles A British biblical scholar who translated and published "The Book of Enoch" in

1906. Charles asserted that Enoch was "built upon the debris of" an older Noah saga than that in Genesis, suggesting that **Enoch's Aramaic traditions might predate the canonical Genesis narrative**.

Saint Ignatius of Antioch (107AD)

Disciple of Saint John the Apostle direct quote:

"It is out of place to confess Jesus Christ and yet Judaize. **For Christianity did not place faith in Judaism, but Judaism placed faith in Christianity**, so that every believing tongue might be gathered together to God."

1 Enoch is Inspired Support

These authors cited or referenced 1 Enoch with great respect, sometimes even calling it "Scripture".

Tertullian (c. 160–220 AD):
(On the "Apparel of Women", Book 1, Chapter 3) direct quote:
"I am aware that the Scripture of Enoch… is not received by some, **because it is not admitted into the Jewish canon either**. I suppose they did not think that, having been published before the deluge, it could have safely survived that worldwide calamity. If that is the reason… let them remember that Noah, the survivor of the deluge, was the great-grandson of Enoch." **Tertullian explicitly defends Enoch as canonical Scripture written by Enoch. He claimed Enoch was only rejected because it contained prophecies of Christ that Judaism rejected.**

Clement of Alexandria (150–215 AD):
Frequently quoted 1 Enoch. One of his students, Origen, also referenced it, although Origen stopped short of calling it scripture due to rising opposition, it's possible he viewed it as divinely inspired and written by Enoch.

Irenaeus of Lyons (130–202 AD):
In "Against Heresies", refers to the "Book of Enoch" when describing the origin of evil spirits, showing it was used in study.

Athenagoras of Athens (around 200 AD)
"A Plea for the Christians"
Wrote about the origin of demons from the "angels who fell from heaven and lusted after women," which parallels 1 Enoch. He doesn't quote Enoch directly but clearly draws on its content.

Lactantius (c. 250–325 AD):
Referenced the fallen angels and the corruption of mankind as described in Enoch in Divine Institutes. Showing Enoch is important for understanding biblical narratives by early Christians.

CHAPTER 8
Juda vs Israel

Juda Vs Israel

In this chapter we will discuss the difference between the start of Juda (Judaism) and Israel (Christianity) before the birth of Christ.

Jeremaiah 3:11 - (KJV) "And the LORD said unto me, the backsliding **Israel hath justified herself more than treacherous Judah**." Stating that Judah was worse than Israel in the eyes of God, and showing a distinct difference between Israel and Judah.

Revelation 3:9 (GNV) "Behold, I will make them of the **Synagogue of Satan, which call themselves Jews**, and are not, but do lie: behold, I say, I will make them that they shall come and worship before thy feet and shall know that I have loved thee." Here we see Jesus saying **Judaism are liars, likely by denying Christ and corrupting Biblical teachings**.

Israel was split into two parts after the death of King Solomon
Judah (Cannan), was the southern kingdom, named after the tribe of Judah. The capital was Jerusalem.
Israel, the northern kingdom, was made up of ten of the twelve tribes of Israel. The capital was Samaria.

The Northern Kingdom was called Israel and comprised the tribes of Reuben, Simeon, Manasseh, Issachar, Zebulun, Ephraim, Dan, Asher, Naphtali and Gad. The Southern Kingdom was called Judah and included the tribes of Judah and Benjamin and the Levites.

1 Kings 11:31 (KJV) "And he said to Jeroboam, Take thee ten pieces: for thus saith the LORD, the God of Israel, Behold, I will rend the kingdom out of the hand of Solomon, and will give ten tribes to thee:"

The northern Kingdom of Israel was destroyed around 720 BCE, when it was conquered by the Neo-Assyrian Empire. Its ten tribes were scattered and never again lived as one people. **The Kingdom of Judah (Canaan) remained intact during this time, and it became a client state of first the Neo-Assyrian Empire.**

Juda Vs Israel

The exilic period saw the development of the Israelite religion towards a monotheistic Judaism, the same one we see today. There is evidence suggesting that some people in the **northern Kingdom of Israel continued to secretly worship their original God (Christ), and could have held onto Enoch's teachings**, when the Assyrian Empire conquered Israel (specifically the northern kingdom) in 722 BCE.

2 Kings 17:18-19 KJV
"Therefore the Lord was very angry with Israel, and removed them out of his sight: there was none left but the tribe of Judah only. **Also Judah kept not the commandments of the Lord their God, but walked in the statutes of Israel which they made."**

The Neo-Assyrian people primarily spoke Aramaic. The ancient people of Judah (Canaan), also known as Judeans spoke Hebrew. In this point in history, it seems the teachings of what would become the Torah would have started having various differences between the sects. Juda having an interpretation similar to modern Judaism. It's possible the people in the Northern Kingdom followed the Aramaic traditions of the coming Messiah in 1 Enoch, that were much more ancient in origin.

The Neo Assyrians would become Christians generations later. The Neo Assyrians worshipped a pantheon of gods in ancient times until their gradual **conversion to Christianity between the 1st and 5th centuries. The Book of Enoch was still included in the biblical scriptures and wasn't removed until around 5th century AD**.

Canaan Became Judea

The region of Canaan, later known as Judea, was officially renamed by around 500 BC. which was about 200 years after the other ten tribes of Israel were conquered by the Neo-Assyrians.

Cannan was named after the "The Canaanites" they were known by their worship of fallen gods, (Ba'al, Molech), child sacrifice, and bearing giants within their bloodline.

Genesis 10:15-19 lists Canaan's descendants, many of whom were known for idolatry, human sacrifice, and ties to the Nephilim bloodline.

Sidon (Phoenicians) – Worshiped Baal (The Bull) associated with fallen angels.
Heth (Hittites) – Later seen as Nephilim, Giants, or even hybrid warriors in biblical texts.
Jebusites (Jerusalem's original inhabitants) – Opposed Israel and had Nephilim/Giant connections.
Amorites – Specifically linked to Nephilim/Giants ("whose height was like the height of the cedars, and he was strong as the oaks;" Amos 2:9 KJV).

Girgasites, Hivites, Arkites, Sinites, Arvadites, Zemarites, Hamathites – Many had ties to **Rephaim** (giant clans).

The Bible records instances where Israelites adopted Canaanite religious practices, including the worship of Baal and rituals associated with Molech. These practices were considered abominable and led to severe consequences. For example, 2 Kings 16:3 mentions **King Ahaz of Judah** engaging in such practices. He even sacrificed his son in the fire, following the detestable ways of the nations the Lord had driven out before the Israelites.

Canaan Became Judea

Archaeological evidence supports these accounts. Excavations in areas like Carthage, a Phoenician colony linked to the Canaanites, have uncovered cemeteries known as "tophets," containing urns with the cremated remains of infants, suggesting ritual child sacrifice. They had similar pottery styles, architectural designs, and inscriptions indicate a shared cultural heritage. **This evidence suggests that the Israelites did not entirely displace the Canaanites but rather emerged from within this cultural context, gradually developing a distinct identity.**

The historical records indicate that the religious and cultural practices of Judea were deeply influenced by Canaanite traditions. Understanding these connections provides valuable insights into the evolution of religious thought in ancient Judaism.

If Aramaic was the primary language of the other ten tribes, why were the scriptures written in Hebrew?

The most likely answer is, Judea took the original Aramaic teaching from the other ten tribes of Israel and rewrote them into Hebrew to fit their own narrative, one mixed with Canaanite teachings, and they removed some books all together like 1 Enoch.

This could be why we see texts like 1 Enoch found in Aramaic not Hebrew, showing it is possible there were Enochian Christians that had a different view of the Torah than Judaism.

It's also important to note modern Judaism follows the Talmud which is their Holy Bible. The Talmud contains several anti-Christian statements like:
Gitten 57a - Which claims Yeshua (Jesus Christ) is in Hell boiling in excrement.

The Talmudic texts mock the Messiah, His mother and His followers (Christians).

Modern Jews Have Canaanite Genetics

Ancient DNA (aDNA) from Canaanite remains (e.g. in Sidon, 3,700 years old) has been sequenced. Modern populations in the Levant, Lebanese, Palestinians, Druze, Sephardic Jews, and some Ashkenazi Jews—all show genetic continuity with those Canaanites.

Genetic studies show that modern Jews, retain Middle Eastern ancestry. That ancestry would include both ancient Israelites and Canaanite, since the two groups shared a common regional gene pool.

A comprehensive 2020 study published in Cell analyzed ancient DNA from 73 individuals excavated at Canaanite sites across present-day Israel and Jordan. The researchers compared this ancient DNA to that of modern populations and found that **both Jewish and Arab groups in the region inherit more than half of their ancestry from these ancient Canaanite populations**.

This finding is corroborated by additional research from Tel Aviv University, and a-crossed multiple other research groups. Which concluded that modern-day Jews share a strong genetic link to the ancient Canaanites.

We don't have DNA from a labeled "tribe of Judah" grave. but we do have samples from the Levantine region and Judahite-period sites. In a nut shell, the same genetic evidence that the modern Jews use to link their ancestry for Judea is the same evidence that links them directly to being Canaanite's.

The genetic evidence matters because of their claim to be of the "Tribe of Judea". Unlike most modern religious practices, their bloodline has a direct root in their faith and belief system.

Modern Judaism consider themselves to be God's chosen people. The Canaanites also considered themselves to be the people of El (god).

El was the high god, the creator, and often referred to as "El Elyon" (God Most High) a title that also appears in the Hebrew Bible (Genesis 14:18–22).

Nazarenes Vs Pharisees

Before Christ: The Pre-Messianic Nazarenes

Long before the birth of Jesus, there existed a community often overlooked by mainstream religious history, it was the ancient Nazarenes, rooted not in the Temple-centered Judaism of Jerusalem, but in a much older, purer tradition that preserved the Aramaic teachings of Enoch, Noah, and the early patriarchs. This pre-Mosaic faith was not centered on sacrifice or the Levitical priesthood, but on direct communion with God, righteousness, visions, and spiritual law, principles clearly seen in texts like 1 Enoch and the Book of Jubilees, which circulated widely among Aramaic-speaking sects.

These proto-Nazarenes believed in a coming Messiah, a suffering servant and heavenly Son of Man, as detailed in Aramaic texts like 1 Enoch 46–48, long before Jesus appeared. Their community structure, rules of conduct, and spiritual focus were radically different from the Pharisaic and Sadducean interpretations of the Torah, which were later institutionalized in Rabbinic Judaism. The Aramaic language itself, spoken by these communities and preserved in the Targums, served as a linguistic bridge to an older, pre-Judaic understanding of divine truth.

After Christ: The Nazarene Assembly and Continuation of Faith After the resurrection of Jesus, the Nazarenes emerged clearly as the first followers of the Messiah, not as a sect of Judaism, but as the continuation of a divine tradition that predated both Moses and the Temple. These believers did not align with the Temple sacrifices or Rabbinic legalism. Instead, they followed Yeshua the Nazarene, who fulfilled the ancient prophecies preserved by Enochian and Aramaic believers.

John 18:19-21 GNV

"The high Priest then asked Jesus of his disciples, and of **his doctrine**,
Jesus answered him, I spake openly to the world: I ever taught in the Synagogue and in the Temple, whither the Jews resort continually, and in secret have I said nothing. Why askest thou me? ask them which heard me what I said unto them: behold, they know what I said."

The High Priest questions Jesus about His doctrine. Showing the Jesus from Nazareth had a different doctrine associated with the scriptures.

Nazarenes Vs Pharisees

Acts 24:5 GNV
"Certainly we have found this man a pestilent fellow, and a mover of sedition among all the Jews throughout the world, and a chief maintainer of the sect of the Nazarenes:"
Paul was accused by the Ananias the High Priest of being the leader of the Nazarenes, showing they had a separate doctrine from Temple Judaism.

The Book of Acts and early Christian writings describe the Nazarenes as followers of "the Way," a term that predates formal Christianity and reflects an inner, spiritual path rooted in Enoch, Noah, and Melchizedek. They continued speaking and teaching in Aramaic, using texts such as the Targum and likely retaining older scriptures not found in the Masoretic canon.

The Nazarenes rejected the authority of the Temple priests, whom Jesus called a "brood of vipers" and taught that the true Temple was not in Jerusalem, but within the human spirit. Their practices included baptism, spiritual gifts, communal living, and prophecy, all of which echo Essene and Enochian customs more than the ritualism of Mosaic Judaism.

Early Church Fathers such as Epiphanius and Jerome noted that the Nazarenes accepted both Jesus as the Messiah and the Torah, but interpreted the Law spiritually, not legally. They did not perform animal sacrifice because Christ was the sacrifice.

John 11:47-48 GNV
"Then gathered the high Priests, and the Pharisees a council, and said, What shall we do? For this man doeth many miracles.
If we let him thus alone, all men will believe in him, and the Romans will come and take away both our place, and the nation."

This verse shows the allegiance between Judaism and Roman government to hide, suppress, or stop the teaching of Christ.

The page below illustrates how we believe the religious evolution went.

Evolution of Religious Teachings

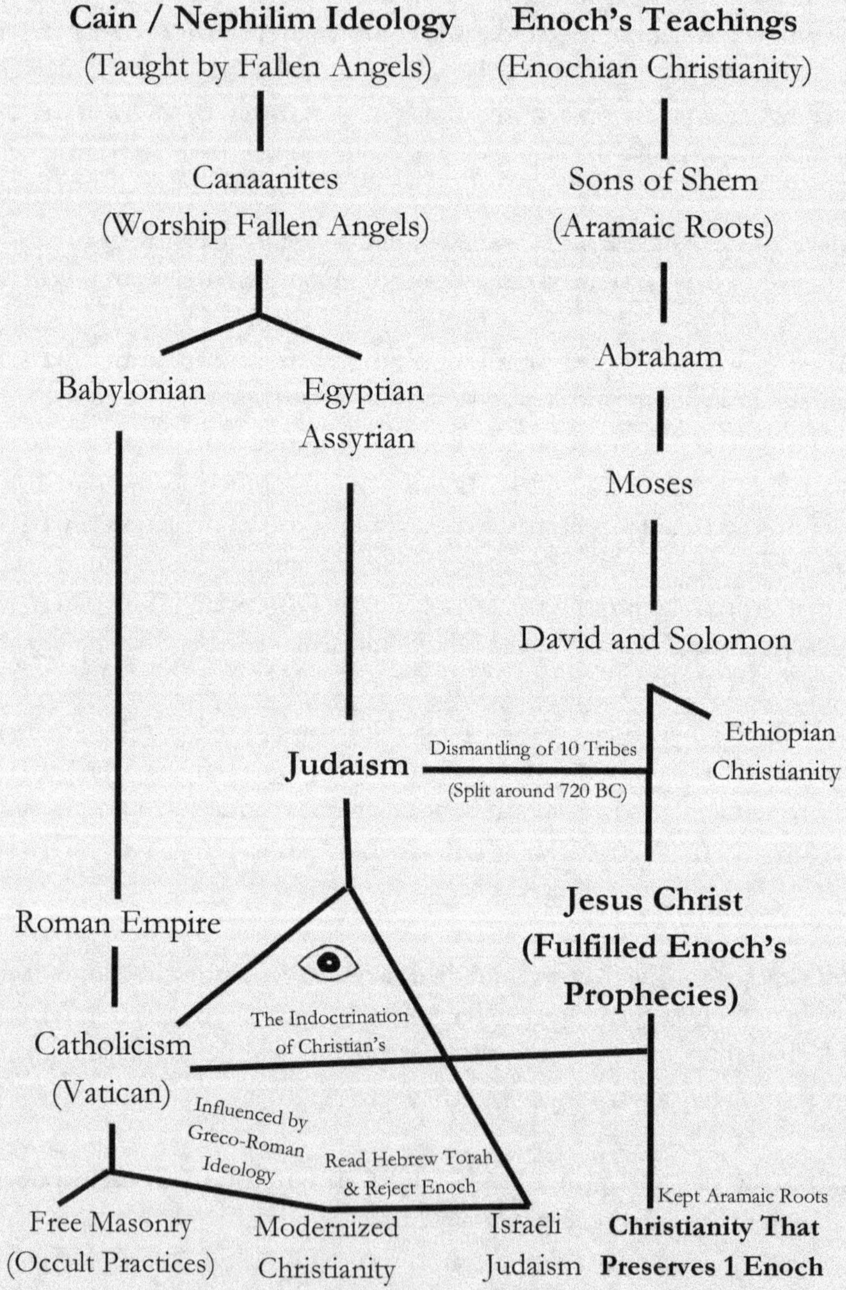

CHAPTER 9
Islam

Islam's Connection to Aramaic

Islam was likely influenced by Aramaic Christianity.

Aramaic was the lingua franca of the region before the advent of Arabic. According to Islamic belief, the divine language directly from God to mankind is Arabic. Arabic is used for prayer and religious study. **A large portion of the Arabic language, including the alphabet, comes from Aramaic.**
Prior to the Arab Islamic Conquest in the 7th century AD, the bulk of the population were Arameans.

The Qu'ran was not composed in isolation but interacted with Aramaic Christian traditions. Arabia had strong Syriac Christian influences. Many of Muhammad's contemporaries, such as the Hanifs (monotheists rejecting polytheism), were possibly exposed to Syriac Christian texts.

Pre-Islamic religious terms were borrowed from Syriac. Key Islamic concepts like salat (prayer) and furqan (deliverance) have Aramaic-Christian origins.

The Qu'ran itself acknowledges foreign words – Surah 16:103 states, "And We certainly know that they say, 'It is only a human being who teaches him.' The tongue of the one they refer to is foreign, while this (Qu'ran) is in clear Arabic." This suggests an awareness of non-Arabic linguistic influence.

Many Qu'ranic passages parallel Syriac hymns, both in structure and meaning. The "Light Verse" (Qu'ran 24:35) and Syriac Christian Hymns relate.
The famous verse: "Allah is the Light of the heavens and the earth. His light is like a niche in which is a lamp…" closely resembles Syriac Christian hymns that describe Christ as the Light of the World. In Syriac, Christ is often referred to as: Nur d'Alma" (Light of the World)

Islam's Connection to Aramaic

The imagery of a lamp, oil, and divine illumination is common in Christian Aramaic poetry. The "Houris" (Quranic Virgins) as Aramaic Beings, The Qu'ran describes houris as heavenly virgins awaiting the faithful in paradise. Luxenberg argues that the word ḥūr (حُوُر) is actually from Syriac ܚܘܪܐ (ḥawra), meaning "pure" or "luminous".

In this reading, paradise does not contain virgins but rather "pure, radiant beings", in line with Syriac Christian descriptions of the afterlife as in the "Blessed Virgin" and Christian Marian Hymns. The Qu'ran highly reveres Mary, mother of Jesus Christ, drawing from Syriac Christian traditions. Syriac hymns from the Peshitta and Ephrem the Syrian celebrate Mary in ways that appear reflected in Qu'ranic descriptions.

Some scholars believe up to 25% of the Qu'ranic texts could come from Aramaic Christian Writings. This could show evidence that all Abrahamic religions (Judaism, Christianity and Islam) all stem from one ancient Aramaic Root religion.

Islam calls Idris (Enoch) a man of truth, The Qur'an mentions Idris (Enoch) briefly but with significant reverence. Qur'an 19:56–57 (Surah Maryam) "And mention Idris in the Book; indeed, he was a man of truth and a prophet. And We raised him to a high station."

This "raising" parallels the biblical statement in Genesis 5:24 KJV that "Enoch walked with God, and he was not, for God took him."

The Tafsir, mentions Enoch being the "the first to write with a pen."

1 Enoch Connection: While not detailed in the Qur'an, the story of Harut and Marut. echoes some Watcher themes. These angels are said to have descended to Earth, taught forbidden knowledge like the use of magic. and were punished, very similar to 1 Enoch's fallen angels (watchers).

Hermes Trismegistus (in Islamic esotericism and Hermeticism), They claim the prophet Enoch as a bridge between divine knowledge and humanity.

Islamic Mysticism

Sufism (Islamic Mysticism) arose in a region where Aramaic was still actively spoken during the early Islamic centuries. Syriac (a dialect of Aramaic) was the liturgical and scholarly language of Eastern Christianity and Jewish communities throughout Mesopotamia, Persia, and Syria. Many early Islamic mystics, especially in Iraq, Persia, and the Levant, encountered Aramaic-speaking monks, scribes, and spiritual teachers.

Sufi mysticism, often portrayed as the heart of Islam, holds an esoteric vision of divine unity, spiritual transformation, and hidden knowledge. While Sufism developed within the Islamic world, its deeper roots may stretch further back, to a lineage of ancient Semitic mysticism embedded in Aramaic traditions, especially those preserved in the Book of Enoch and the Targum of Job. These texts, rich with themes of angelic hierarchies, inner illumination, and celestial ascent, share striking similarities with Sufi cosmology and practice.

Sufism emphasizes the inner journey toward God through purification of the soul (tazkiyah), remembrance (dhikr), and direct experience (ma'rifah). Similarly, the Aramaic Targums, 1 Enoch, and Dead Sea Scrolls highlight heavenly journeys, visions, and the idea of walking in righteousness. Think of Enoch's ascent or Daniel's visions, both mystical and internal as well as cosmic.

The Light Within (Divine Illumination)

Sufi – Rumi:
"The wound is the place where the Light enters you."

Targum Job 29:3
"When His lamp shone over my head, and by His light I walked through darkness."

1 Enoch 5:7 (Charles)
"But for the elect there shall be light and joy and peace, And they shall inherit the earth"

All 3 texts describe "The light of God" as both guidance and inner transformation.

Islamic Mysticism

Divine Justice and the Unseen Order

Sufi – Rumi:
"Don't grieve. Anything you lose comes round in another form."

Targum Job 1:21
"The Lord gave and the Lord has taken away. May the name of the Lord be blessed."

1Enoch 94:1 (Charles)
"And now I say unto you, my sons, love righteousness and walk therein; For the paths of righteousness are worthy of acceptation, But the paths of unrighteousness shall suddenly be destroyed and vanish."

All 3 texts speak on acceptance of divine will, the ephemeral nature of worldly things, and the hidden justice of God. central to both Job's journey and Sufi sur render.

Sufism is far from being isolated within Islam, it may in fact be a surviving branch of an older, Semitic mystical tradition, one encoded in Aramaic texts like 1 Enoch and Targum Jonathan. These writings preserve a vision of divine intimacy, angelic knowledge, and cosmic ascent that predates both Islam and Rabbinic Judaism. Their survival in hidden sects, Essenes, early Christians, mystic Jews, may have subtly shaped the Sufi worldview.

By tracing these echoes, we recover not just theological parallels but a spiritual lineage, one that stretches from Enoch's heavenly journeys and Job's trials through the deserts of Aramaic-speaking prophets, and into the heart of Sufi poetry and vision.

CHAPTER 10
Zoroastrianism

Zoroastrianism

Zoroastrianism likely emerged between 1800 and 1200 BC, making it over 3000 years old and possibly the oldest continuous monotheistic religion in history. Christianity and Zoroastrianism share several key similarities, many of which suggest possible historical influences.

Monotheism.
Zoroastrianism believes in One God.
Christianity believes in One God.

Messianic Figure.
Zoroastrianism predicts a future savior, the Saoshyant, who will bring resurrection and defeat evil.
Christianity believes Jesus Christ is the Messiah Who will return in the end times and will bring resurrection and defeat evil.

Virgin Birth Messiah.
Zoroastrianism – The prophecy states that the seed of Zoroaster is preserved in the lake, and a virgin will miraculously conceive after coming into contact with it.
Christianity - Jesus is born of the Virgin Mary by the power of the Holy Spirit, then later baptized in a river.

Final Judgment & Resurrection.
Zoroastrianism believes in a final judgment where the righteous are rewarded and the wicked are punished. The dead will be resurrected.
Christianity also teaches a final judgment, resurrection of the dead, and eternal destinies in heaven or hell.

Concept of Heaven and Hell.
Zoroastrianism believes souls are judged at death; the righteous go to paradise, and the wicked suffer in darkness until the final purification.
Christianity believes souls are judged and sent to heaven or hell, with a final resurrection and judgment at the end of time.

Zoroastrianism

Free Will and Moral Choice.
Zoroastrianism teaches a cosmic battle between good and evil, where humans must choose between truth and deceit.
Christianity emphasizes free will and moral responsibility in choosing between God and sin.

Angelic Beings and Demonic Forces.
Zoroastrianism features divine beings (Amesha Spentas, Yazatas) who assist God, and demonic forces led by Angra Mainyu.
Christianity recognizes angels serving God, and demonic forces led by Satan (a fallen angel).

All of this shows us a direct connection to Zoroastrian and Christian Belief.
Most scholars argue Zoroastrian teachings far pre-date Judaism.
That is correct, but it does not pre-date Enoch's teachings from the pre-flood world.

There is a strong visual connection between the **ancient Zoroastrian Faravahar symbol and the modern Aramean-Syriac flag**. Both use winged shapes with a central figure or image—Faravahar shows a man inside a winged disc, while the Aramean-Syriac flag has a flame or star rising from between the wings. Even though the designs are different, they share the same basic idea: something powerful or divine rising or guiding from the center. This design could represent Christ, the flame or light at the center, rising above and carried by heavenly forces.

Both symbols point to a deeper message about being lifted up, guided from above, or connected to something higher. These ideas match what we find in the teachings of Enochian Christianity, where angels, light, and heavenly journeys are key themes. The Arameans, who spoke the language of the early prophets and preserved texts like 1 Enoch, may have passed down symbols that later influenced other cultures—possibly even early Zoroastrianism. The similar look of these two symbols may be more than coincidence; it could be a sign of shared roots in an ancient faith that once stretched from the Middle East into Persia.

The Japhetic Echo

Zoroastrianism could represent a Japhethic reflection of Enochian Christianity.

While much attention is given to Shem's descendants (including the Hebrews, Assyrians, and Arameans), this chapter explores a lesser-known but critical branch: the Japhetic echo, which is the transmission of Enochian knowledge through Japheth, Noah's eldest son, which would later manifest as the moral and cosmological system of Zoroastrianism.

Genesis 10:2 (KJV) lists the sons of Japheth as, "Gomer, Magog, **Madai**, Javan, Tubal, Meshech, and Tiras."

Zoroastrians most likely come from Japheth, particularly through his son **Madai,** the ancestor of the Medes, an ancient Iranian people who played a foundational role in the rise of Persia. This means their teachings could have originated from Enoch.
Noah, who "found favor in the eyes of the Lord," (Genesis 6:8 ESV) would have preserved Enoch's writings. Enoch was Noah's great grandfather and surely, he would have shared the first scribe's teachings with his sons!

After the flood, Noah's sons divided the earth.
Japheth was granted the northern and eastern territories, a wide expanse covering what would become Anatolia, the Caucasus, Persia, India, and parts of Europe.

While Shem remained central to the development of Aramaic-speaking communities, Japheth's descendants carried fragments of Noah's teachings, originally delivered in Aramaic, into the eastern regions.

The Japhetic Echo

The Avestan language (used in Zoroastrian scriptures) **shares grammatical structures and phonetic parallels with both early Aramaic** and Sanskrit. This suggests that the core cosmological ideas may have a common linguistic and theological ancestor, **pointing to Aramaic as a unifying origin**.

Zarathustra, though writing in Avestan, speaks of divine wisdom passed down from the "first man" and a world corrupted by a deceiving spirit. He brings a message of righteousness, judgment, and hope for renewal, which are key themes in 1 Enoch, especially in the Aramaic fragments found among the Dead Sea Scrolls.

The Japhetic echo is an essential piece of the Aramaic Roots puzzle. It shows that Enochian truth was not exclusive to Semitic lines, but universal, intended to reach every corner of the post-Flood world.

While Zoroastrianism developed independently in many ways, its foundational structures are too deeply aligned with Aramaic Roots and Enochian thought to be ignored.

Zoroastrian's Believed in Christ

The Three Wise Men or **Magi** who visited the Baby Jesus in Matthew 2:1-12 were likely **Zoroastrian** priests from Persia. The Greek word used in Matthew 2:1 for wise men is "μάγοι" (Magoi), which refers to the priestly class of Zoroastrianism in Persia.

The Magi followed a star to find Jesus (Matthew 2:2)
Zoroastrians believed in a coming Saoshyant (Savior) and looked for celestial signs of his arrival. The Persian priesthood **closely studied the stars, linking astronomy with divine prophecy,** much like 1 Enoch.

The Magi brought gold, frankincense, and myrrh (Matthew 2:11).
Gold was worn by Zoroastrian priests. Fire temples were adorned in gold, symbolizing purity.
Frankincense was a key element in Zoroastrian fire temple rituals.
Myrrh was used in Zoroastrian burial rites, possibly foreshadowing Jesus death and resurrection.

The Magi in Matthew 2 were almost certainly Zoroastrian priests from Persia. Their title, star prophecy, connection to pre-christ messianic expectations, and ritual gifts all point to Zoroastrian influence. This suggests a deep Persian-Jewish-Christian connection to traditions linking back to these Aramaic Roots.

The Dead Sea Scrolls contain apocalyptic themes similar to Zoroastrian eschatology.

1 Enoch and Zoroastrianism both emphasize angelic rebellion, a final judgment, and resurrection, suggesting possible cross-influence. If Enochian traditions predate the Exile, it is possible that Zoroastrian beliefs were influenced by earlier Aramaic traditions rather than the other way around.

Tobit written around 200 BC in Aramaic **reflects Persian and Semitic Cross influence**. The angel Raphael resembles a Zoroastrian guardian spirit. The demon Asmodeus (Tobit 3:8) has a name linked to the Persian demon Aeshma.

Zoroastrian's Believed in Christ

If Noah preserved Enoch's writings, his descendants (especially those migrating eastward) may have passed them to early Persian cultures. This could explain why Zoroastrianism and 1 Enoch texts share common themes, including prophecies of the coming of Christ.

If Enoch's writings influenced early Persian beliefs, the Saoshyant may be an adaptation of the Enochian Messiah. With the direct link in the bible to the wise men being Zoroastrian, it's very likely they believed in the coming of Christ even in ancient times.

Daniel's Connection to Zoroastrianism.
Daniel was taken captive to Babylon, but lived long enough to serve under the Persian Empire, especially under King Darius and Cyrus the Great. Zoroastrianism was the dominant religion of the Achaemenid Persian Empire, founded by Zarathustra (Zoroaster). This places Daniel right in the timeframe and geography of Zoroastrian rise and influence.

Daniel was appointed over all the "wise men" (magoi) of Babylon and Persia (Daniel 2:48). The term "Magi" later referred to Zoroastrian priests.

Daniel may have trained or influenced the Magi, meaning his apocalyptic and messianic teachings could have been preserved in Persian religious circles, possibly explaining why the Magi from the East came looking for the Messiah. This could show a connection between 1 Enoch, Daniel in the Old Testament, and Zoroastrian Belief.

Daniel may have acted as a bridge between the Aramaic tradition of Enoch and the emerging Zoroastrian thought of the Persians. His high status among the Magi and presence during Zoroastrianism's rise makes him a likely transmitter of Enochian Christian thought into Persian religious circles, which then influenced both Zoroastrianism and modern Christian eschatology.

CHAPTER 11
Ancient Sumerian

Ancient Sumerian

Sumerian was written using the cuneiform script, one of the earliest systems of writing on earth. Sumerian is considered a **language isolate**, meaning it has no known relatives or established connection to any other language family.

It's known as early as the 4th millennium BCE. It is associated with the Sumerian civilization, which is credited with establishing some of the first cities, such as Uruk and Ur. In Sumerian texts, the Sumerian language was often associated with divine origins. The gods in Sumerian texts, particularly Enki, were said to have given humans language and writing.

This matches up with 1 Enoch 8:1-4 account of the fallen angels (gods) giving mankind knowledge. In certain Sumerian texts, it's portrayed as the original, pure language before linguistic confusion occurred.
Our theory is: this is the language of the fallen angels, (Sons of God, Watchers).

The cuneiform system used for Sumerian was later adapted for other languages, including Akkadian, but many of the original signs and conventions were retained. Akkadian-speaking priests and scribes continued using Sumerian in religious ceremonies and incantations, reinforcing its divine status.

Akkadian stands as a crucial link in the evolution of Semitic languages. It is widely accepted that Hebrew and Aramaic both evolved from an earlier common language. Akkadian was written in cuneiform script. The best-known version of The Epic of Gilgamesh was written in this ancient cuneiform.

Akkadian offers a window into the ancient world that set the stage for later developments in Mesopotamia. It is a **language that influenced the formative periods of Hebrew and Aramaic**. This background helps explain why certain concepts, narrative techniques, or even linguistic features appear in the Bible. While Sumerian is viewed as the language of ancient gods (fallen angels), in Mesopotamian tradition, Aramaic is often seen as the language of divine revelation in monotheistic traditions.

Ancient Sumerian

There is interconnectedness of Ancient Texts. The similarities between literary and religious texts across Mesopotamian, Akkadian and later Biblical Hebrew suggest that ideas and linguistic forms were transmitted across cultures. This supports theories that some traditions in the Bible might have roots in earlier Mesopotamian or Aramaic contexts rather than originating purely within a later Hebrew framework.

Biblical critics have doubted the existence of writing before the time of Moses. But recently Archaeologists have unearthed an ancient library in the city of Ur that may prove their theory to be false. This library contains thousands of stone "books" that were most likely written in cuneiform and later in Akkadian.

Ur of Chaldees was Abraham's home before he moved to Caanan, and some of these books were written even before Abraham's day, and a full 1,000 years before Moses was born. The books consist of both scholarly subjects and books that an ordinary tradesman would read. If an ordinary tradesman living 4,000 years ago could read and write, why should we doubt that Enoch who was a scribe would have written his own book, 1st Enoch, copies of which were found in the Dead Sea Scrolls. The writing of 1 Enoch was in Aramaic, showing a possible cover up, that Aramaic may be older than originally thought.

Jubilees Tells Origin of Cuneiform

In this section we will show the connection between Sumerian Cuneiform and Noah in the ancient book of Jubilees.

Book of Jubilees 8:1-4 says: "In the twenty-ninth jubilee, in the first week, in the beginning thereof Arpachshad took to himself a wife and her name was Rasu'eja, the daughter of Susan, the daughter of Elam, and she bare him a son in the third year in this week, and he called his name Kainam. And the son grew, and his father taught him writing, and he went to seek for himself a place where he might seize for himself a city. And he found a writing which former [generations] had carved on the rock, and he read what was thereon, and he **transcribed** it and sinned owing to it; for it contained **the teaching of the Watchers** in accordance with which they used to observe the omens of the sun and moon and stars in all the signs of heaven. And he wrote it down and said nothing regarding it; for he was afraid to speak to **Noah** about it lest he should be **angry** with him on account of it."

Kainam, was from the bloodline of Shem. It's said he wrote down ancient writings of the fallen angels (watchers, gods). It is told before this sin, he was taught ancient writings by his father, Arpachshad, writings which likely included 1 Enoch.

"**Carved on the rock**" is showing us the Sumerian cuneiform chiseled into stone.

"**The Watcher's**" Are said to have carved these ancient tablets, pre-flood. These teachings would survive to this day, being the root of the religious system for Canaanites, later used by the Babylonian's and Assyrian's.

"**Transcribed it**." Showing the use of writing in pre-flood times and Kainam having the ability to write and read this ancient script.

"**Noah** being **angry**". Knowing how great evil was in the pre flood world he escaped.

This not only shows a direct connection to the Sumerian cuneiform being linked to the fallen angels (gods, watchers), it additionally shows that there were written books and records going back to pre-flood times and also shows it is likely that Noah preserved the writings of Enoch, the first scribe.

CHAPTER 12
The Persecution

The Persecution of Enochian Christians

The preservation of 1 Enoch by Armenians and Ethiopians may not be coincidence but divine strategy. Armenia, through Japheth's legacy, and Ethiopia, through Solomon and Sheba's royal-spiritual merger of Ham and Shem's bloodlines, both kept the sacred Enochian teachings alive. Their connection to the Aramaic Roots of Christianity is not just linguistic, but deeply theological, retaining a vision of angelic order, pre-Flood history, and divine judgment rejected in later rabbinic Judaism and Greco-Roman Christianity.

In both nations, Enoch was not a legend, but a prophet. His book was not apocrypha, but truth, and the language that carried his visions, Aramaic, was the thread that wove together the earliest form of God's revelation to mankind, long before modern religion. Both these groups suffered horrible persecution.

The Armenian Genocide: this tragic event resulted in the **deaths of an estimated 1.5 million Armenians, the vast majority of whom were Christians.** and the mass displacement of survivors.

This tragic event not only reduced the population but also resulted in the destruction and dispersal of cultural and religious assets, **manuscripts, liturgical texts, and theological commentaries were often lost** or **deliberately suppressed during and after the genocid**e. The genocide and subsequent dispersion of the Armenian people meant that many repositories of ancient knowledge were scattered. Manuscripts that might have contained original or early versions of apocalyptic texts, or commentaries on Enochian teachings, were lost in the chaos of mass migration, violence, and cultural destruction.

Genocide Acknowledgment: In 2015, the Armenian Parliament officially recognized the genocide of the **Arameans (Syriacs)** perpetrated by the Ottoman Empire during World War I, alongside the Armenian and Greek genocides. **This acknowledgment reflects a recognition of shared suffering and a historical bond between the two peoples.**

This shows not only another similarity between the Arameans and the Armenians but is also clear evidence that both groups were targeted for their matching beliefs.

The Persecution of Enochian Christians

Armenian Christians: apart from the catastrophic events of the 20th century, Armenian Christians have faced centuries of persecution under varying regimes (from Ottoman policies to Soviet suppression). This continuous adversity has often resulted in the loss or censoring of texts that did not align with official religious or political views. As a part of their broader religious heritage, the distinctive mystical and apocalyptic elements, closely tied to the original Enochian traditions, were sometimes sidelined or lost amid efforts to forge a unified national identity under external pressures.

Ethiopian Christians: similarly, Ethiopian Christians have experienced periods of persecution and marginalization. In modern times, political instability, religious conflict, and pressures from regional powers have affected their ability to maintain historical traditions. While the Ethiopian Orthodox Tewahedo Church still honors 1 Enoch, academic and popular understanding of the broader Enochian teachings has sometimes suffered due to isolation, conflict, and cultural suppression.

The Arabic Slave Trade: from the early medieval period through the modern era, parts of Ethiopia were subject to the broader dynamics of the Arab slave trade. While the trade itself was multi-faceted and involved various regions along the Red Sea and in the interior of Africa, Ethiopian Christians sometimes found themselves caught in systems of coercion and marginalization. This trade, along with related military and economic pressures, **had social, religious and cultural impacts on the communities involved**.

Both Armenians and Ethiopians, were custodians of Enochian Christian traditions and they have encountered significant cultural disruptions that interfered with the direct transmission of early teachings. The loss of documents and a break in scholarly tradition have meant that parts of the original Enochian vision may never have been fully recovered. Although the evidence is clear, these groups were guardians of ancient sacred knowledge and were heavily persecuted for it.

The Persecution by Greece: Hellenization

Hellenization and the Erasure of Aramaic-Early Christian Memory.

Hellenization refers to the spread and adoption of Greek culture, language, religion, philosophy, and political systems across the regions conquered by Alexander the Great and his successors, beginning in the 4th century BC.

The rise of Hellenization was not merely a cultural evolution, it was a calculated attempt to **overwrite the sacred memory and divine order established in the earliest days of covenantal history**. Hellenization represented more than the adoption of Greek language, architecture, or political models. It was a **spiritual invasion**, a force that sought to uproot the foundational truths preserved through Enoch, Noah, and Shem, transmitted through an Aramaic-speaking lineage that long predated Mosaic legalism and later Jewish tradition.

In the time of the Maccabees, this ideological battle came to a head. The Seleucid Empire, under Antiochus IV Epiphanes, enforced Hellenistic religion and customs upon the Jewish population. Circumcision was banned, the Sabbath was profaned, and the Temple in Jerusalem was desecrated with pagan sacrifices. These were acts that mirrored the very transgressions condemned in the Book of Enoch. The faithful were faced with a stark choice: embrace the spirit of Greek enlightenment or hold fast to the ancestral ways rooted in divine revelation. The Maccabean resistance, then, was more than political rebellion, it was a defense of a pre-Mosaic, pre-rabbinic expression of righteousness that preserved the sacred order first revealed to the patriarchs and prophets.

The Maccabean revolt was sparked in part by the **rejection of Hellenization,** aligning them with groups trying to preserve ancient, possibly pre-Mosaic Enochian traditions. The Maccabees likely spoke Aramaic. Aramaic was widely used during the Maccabean period.

The Persecution by Greece: Hellenization

In the context of the Maccabees/Arameans, Hellenization meant:

- Imposing Greek customs on Semitic societies (gymnasiums, Greek dress).
- Replacing Aramaic with Greek language and texts.
- Forcing Jews / Arameans to abandon the Torah and Targums.
- Introducing pagan worship (Zeus, sacrifice of pigs in the Temple).

The Maccabees represent a pivot point, a group of religious reformers reacting against foreign corruption and restoring temple-based, possibly ancient traditions. While they may not be fully aligned with the Aramean/Enochian sects, their actions made space for Enochian groups like the Essenes to flourish, and those groups directly preserved 1 Enoch.

Notice the similarities to "Hellen-ization" and the word "Heathen-ization" or in proper "Heathenize". Heathenism is the Pagan Religion. While Heathen (ethnikos) in the bible generally refers to Pagans and Gentiles.

We see in this passage possibly before Christ, the ancient Aramaic teachings would have been persecuted heavily. This threat to the original faith did not end with Hellenization.

The Persecution by Rome: Ecclesiastical Subversion

In the first few centuries after Christ's ministry, many Christian groups, especially those expressing apocalyptic visions and mystical experiences, faced persecution from Roman authorities who viewed them as subversive or heretical. Any texts that didn't fit their religious narrative were banned.

During the persecution of Christians by the Roman Empire, it's said that **thousands of Christians were killed or jailed**. Many of these early groups operated in regions where Aramaic was the common language. Their texts, liturgies, and community rules were embedded in the cultural and linguistic context of the Near East. However, state-sponsored persecution often led to the clandestine transmission of these writings, making them vulnerable to loss or alteration.

As Christianity expanded into the Greco-Roman world, a tragic shift occurred. In an effort to distance itself from its Semitic origins, and under pressure to accommodate Roman sensibilities, much of early Christianity began aligning itself with the very structures that had once sought to destroy its foundation. Greco-Roman Christianity adopted Greek philosophical frameworks and Latin ecclesiastical authority, gradually marginalizing the Aramaic texts, traditions, and teachings that had defined the earliest followers of Yeshua (Jesus Christ).

Instead of preserving the Enochian worldview echoed in the teachings of Christ and His apostles with its emphasis on angelic hierarchies, divine judgment, resurrection, and covenantal fidelity, the institutional church began to lean heavily on the emerging rabbinic interpretations of the Hebrew Scriptures. These interpretations, themselves shaped in opposition to early messianic movements, were embraced as theological grounding in a church now estranged from its own Aramaic heritage.

The Persecution by Rome:
Ecclesiastical Subversion

As church authorities gradually moved toward establishing a unified canonical collection, texts that did not align with the emerging Greco-Romain Christian views, like 1 Enoch, were rejected or outright banned.

The persecution of Christians. whether during early Roman times, or later Islamic periods, has directly affected the survival of Aramaic-rooted teachings. These texts and traditions, including apocalyptic literature like 1 Enoch, suffered due to direct suppression and censorship. The fragmentation and loss of vital manuscripts and adaptation pressures altered their original form and meaning.

In reclaiming this ancient foundation, we do not reject Scripture; we restore its context. We do not abandon history; we uncover what history has hidden.
The Aramaic Roots of the faith were never fully lost, only buried beneath layers of cultural sediment.

The Persecution by Islam: The Crusades

Islamic forces took over Christian regions largely through military conquest in the 7th and 8th centuries AD.
The Holy Land, a key religious center for Aramaic Christianity, was taken in 638 AD. Tensions between Muslim rulers and Christian pilgrims, along with the rise of aggressive Islamic powers like the Seljuks, eventually triggered the Crusades, which were Christian military campaigns to reclaim the Holy Land. These Christian responses weren't just battles over land; they were battles over language, scripture, and the preservation of the original faith.

When Islam spread, it didn't just conquer Christian and Jewish lands, it displaced the culture, language, and sacred traditions of those lands. The Qu'ran accuses Jews and Christians of corrupting their scriptures, which justified Muslim rulers restricting or destroying non-Islamic texts, such as Torahs and Targums.

It makes sense Islam would try to erase Jesus Christ's Aramaic Roots, to have a better theological based argument for their texts. During Islamic rule Christians were increasingly harassed or even killed. Reports of church destruction, especially the burning of the Church of the Holy Sepulchre in 1009, shocked the Christian world.

Before Islam, The Holy Land, Syria, and Mesopotamia were still full of Aramaic-speaking Christians.

After Islam, Arabic became the official administrative language of the empire.

Over time, Aramaic dialects like Syriac faded from public use. Christian churches in formerly Aramaic-speaking regions shifted to Arabic Bibles and liturgy, especially after the 9th century. Jewish scholars began writing Judeo-Arabic, Hebrew texts in Arabic script to avoid persecution.

The Persecution by Islam:
The Crusades

There's strong evidence that Islamic rule led to a language shift from Aramaic to Arabic, often through systemic pressure or sometimes even through direct violence. There are documented cases of the destruction or banning of Bibles, Torahs, and possibly Targums, especially during Islamic polemical movements. Many sacred texts likely were either lost, hidden, or translated into Arabic to survive, often altering the way original beliefs were practiced or preserved.

The First Crusade captured Jerusalem in 1099, establishing Christian Crusader States, including the Kingdom of Jerusalem. The capture of Jerusalem was the high point seen as the fulfillment of prophecy and divine justice. Throughout the 1100s the continued survival of Crusader States was viewed as God's ongoing protection.

The Crusaders were Latin Christians from Europe, unfamiliar with the Eastern languages and texts. **They brought Latin Bibles, Roman liturgy, and Western traditions**. The Aramaic-speaking Christians were often marginalized or viewed with suspicion. These communities were pushed to the mountains (Assyria, Lebanon) or wiped out entirely. The "remnant" of Aramaic believers (like the Assyrian Christians, Maronites, hidden sects) survived in isolation, but their scriptures and traditions were largely lost to history.

These Latinized Christians wouldn't have kept 1 Enoch as scripture, since it was rejected by the Roman Church.

Aramaic, the language of Abraham and Jesus Christ Himself was cast out. What remained was Latin Christianity in the West, and Arabic Islam in the East.

The Persecution by USSR: Bolshevik & Ottoman

Just as ancient empires (Babylon, Assyria, Rome) warred against the prophets and righteous, Soviet communism could be seen as a modern empire of seeking to erase the Enochian truth carried by Aramaic-rooted faiths.

Under the Soviet Union: **Estimated Deaths of 12–20 million Christians. (broad estimate, including prison, famine, execution, and gulag deaths)**

Russian Orthodox Church: Thousands of clergy were executed, churches destroyed or repurposed. Between 1917 and 1941, estimates suggest: 45,000–50,000 clergy were killed.

Assyrian, Aramean and Armenian Christians: Massacres and deportations in both Soviet and adjacent Ottoman contexts. Up to 750,000 Assyrians and Armenians may have perished during this broader regional period. These populations may have preserved liturgies, and texts in Aramaic dialects going back to early Enochian Christianity or ancient pre-flood traditions.

Early Bolshevik leadership included a number of secular Jews. Several individuals of Jewish ethnic background played prominent roles in the early Bolshevik Party.

In some departments (like the Cheka), estimates suggest up to 50% of leadership positions were held by ethnic Jews early on. This number is claimed to have declined under Stalin, who purged many religious Jewish Bolsheviks.

Aramaic Speaking or Mystical Jewish communities overall suffered great persecution under the Soviet regime. Estimated Soviet-era deaths specifically due to Bolshevik/Communist actions: 100,000–500,000 religious Jews died.

This erasure of the Aramaic-speaking faith could be viewed as a genocidal attack on divine memory, the "remnant" holding the original message from Adam, Enoch, and Noah.

The Persecution by Nazis: The Holocaust

The Holocaust was not only a humanitarian tragedy but also a cultural and theological eraser. Amidst the targeting of Jewish populations, what may have also been lost were remnants of a distinct Aramaic-speaking tradition, one possibly rooted in Enochian Christianity and preserving ancient texts like 1 Enoch. While mainstream history frames Judaism as a monolith, the reality is more complex: not all who identified as Jews practiced the later, Talmudic form. Some communities may have quietly maintained older beliefs that traced back to the earliest Aramaic traditions.

Nazi ideology, while superficially cloaked in Christian language, was fundamentally opposed to Aramaic-rooted theology. Its obsession with a pure Aryan bloodline aligns more closely with the ancient mythos of the Nephilim than with the humble, Semitic lineage of Adam and Enoch. Ironically, by persecuting the Jewish people, many of whom had already inherited a mixture of Canaanite and post-Exilic influences, the Nazis may have also unknowingly suppressed a minority who still held echoes of the original Aramaic faith.

Libraries, synagogues, and private collections were systematically destroyed or looted. Though records are incomplete, it is likely that some of these held rare Aramaic texts outside the Talmudic canon—possibly even remnants of early Christian or Enochian writings. These were not simply mystical traditions but potentially historical continuities of the original patriarchal belief system.

In the aftermath of the war, scholars attempting to reconstruct pre-rabbinic traditions **found noticeable gaps**. Anecdotal reports from survivors speak of fragmented memories of teachings and customs that no longer had a place in the post-Holocaust religious landscape. Whether these were remnants of Enochian Christianity, Jewish Mysticism, or another form of Aramaic-rooted theology remains unknown. But the Holocaust, beyond its devastating human toll, likely played a role in erasing a lesser known, but theologically significant, strand of ancient belief.

The Persecution by Nazis: The Holocaust

What emerged after the Holocaust, within the surviving Jewish religious communities, was primarily Talmudic Judaism. This branch had long rejected the Aramaic Rooted traditions, most notably the Book of Enoch, the belief in a divine Messiah, and the older Semitic theology that predated rabbinic interpretations. Talmudic Judaism historically has held a deep hatred towards Jesus Christ and early Christianity, making the survival of Aramaic rooted beliefs highly unlikely within its post-war revival. For those seeking to preserve or revive the original Semitic traditions, the devastation of the Holocaust created both a physical and theological void. One in which remnants of the original faith may have been deliberately left buried under the rubble of war.

This erasure, however, was not an isolated incident. Throughout history, Aramaic Roots believers, those holding to the older teachings of Adam, Enoch, and the original Messiah concept. have been caught in the ideological crossfire of larger powers. The Crusaders, like Hitler, often carried the label of Christianity but actively suppressed the Aramaic message at its core. In both cases, the outward religious identity masked a deeper opposition to Enochian Ideology.

Similarly, the 20th century's great ideological empires, Nazism and Soviet Communism, stood on opposing ends of the political spectrum but were united in their hostility toward any tradition rooted in ancient, faith-based authority. Aramaic teachings, were treated as subversive or primitive. The same pattern unfolded centuries earlier: during the Islamic conquests and the medieval Crusades, those who followed Enochian or Nazarene teachings found themselves persecuted, assimilated, or erased.

Across all these periods—Crusades, Islamic expansion, Soviet & Nazi genocide—a recurring pattern emerges: Aramaic Roots traditions were not preserved by empire but often extinguished by it. Whether under the banner of religion or secular ideology, the ancient voices tied to Enoch, the Son of Man, and early Aramaic Christianity were suppressed by every dominant force that followed. The cumulative effect has been a near-total erasure of this ancient faith from the pages of accepted history, an erasure not by accident, but by satanic design.

Chapter 13
Book of Jude and 1 Enoch

Book of Jude and 1 Enoch

Jude 1-2 KJV: "Jude, the **servant of Jesus Christ, and brother of James**, to them that are sanctified by God the Father, and preserved in Jesus Christ, and called: Mercy unto you, and peace, and love, be multiplied."

Jude introduces himself with authority, identifying as both a servant of Jesus Christ and the brother of James, placing himself within Christ's bloodline. This introduction sets the stage for the seriousness and urgency of his message.

Jude 3 KJV: "Beloved, when I gave all diligence to write unto you of the common salvation, it was needful for me to write unto you and exhort you that ye should earnestly contend for the faith **which was once delivered unto the saints**."

Jude originally intended to write a general letter about salvation, but he was compelled, perhaps even prophetically burdened, to address a more urgent issue. His phrase "the faith which was once delivered unto the saints" suggests a primal, ancient faith, one that predates the distortions of later religion. He implies that this foundational truth has been neglected or suppressed and must be recovered and defended.

Jude 4 KJV: "For there are certain **men crept in unawares**, **who were before of old ordained to this condemnation, ungodly men,** turning the grace of our God into lasciviousness, and denying the only Lord God, and our Lord Jesus Christ."

Jude warns that corrupt individuals have infiltrated the faith community — likely referring to groups that have hijacked or distorted true Christianity and its Aramaic roots. These men were "ordained to this condemnation" long ago — a phrase that echoes both Enoch's prophecy against the fallen angels and the ancient enemies of truth. They pervert God's grace into immoral freedom and reject Jesus Christ Himself.

Book of Jude and 1 Enoch

Jude 5 KJV: "**I will therefore put you in remembrance**, though ye once knew this, how that the Lord, having saved the people out of the land of Egypt, afterward destroyed them that believed not."

Jude tells his audience that he is putting the Christians in remembrance, his knowledge isn't new, linking it directly to 1 Enoch that was lost for several generations. He is restoring awareness of ancient truths known to early saints, perhaps even to Adam, Enoch, and Noah. This may also allude to the deliberate removal of Enoch's writings from later canons.

Jude 6 KJV: "**And the angels which kept not their first estate**, but left their own habitation, he hath reserved in everlasting chains under darkness unto the judgment of the great day."

This directly references 1 Enoch 6 and Genesis 6 — the story of the Watchers, angelic beings who abandoned their heavenly station to cohabit with human women. As a result, they were bound in chains and held for future judgment. Jude affirms the reality of this Enochian narrative and places it at the center of his eschatological warning.

Jude 7 KJV: "Even as Sodom and Gomorrah, and the cities about them in like manner, giving themselves over to fornication, and going after **strange flesh**, are set forth for an example, suffering the vengeance of eternal fire."

Jude draws a deliberate parallel between Sodom and Gomorrah and the sins of the Watchers, described earlier in verse 6 and in detail in 1 Enoch. Both cases involve extreme sexual corruption and the pursuit of "strange flesh" — unnatural unions that violate divine order. Importantly, this is the only time Jude names the post-Flood example first before describing similar patterns in the present or past.

By doing this, Jude uses Sodom's destruction as a prophetic signpost, warning that the judgment of the Watchers and of Sodom are connected — part of a continuous pattern of rebellion stretching from the antediluvian age to more recent history. The rest of the letter will follow this same pattern but often without explicitly naming the ancient examples, instead alluding to Enochian themes like corruption, murmuring, arrogance, and blasphemy, traits rooted in the pre-Flood world.

Jude 8 KJV: "Likewise, also these filthy dreamers defile the flesh, despise dominion, and speak evil of dignities."

Jude draws a parallel between ancient sins and the present danger. These "dreamers" — likely mystics, false teachers, or spiritual imposters — follow the same path as the Watchers and Sodom. They defile their bodies, reject divine authority, and blaspheme heavenly beings — behavior described in detail in 1 Enoch as traits of both the fallen angels and their corrupted Nephilim offspring.

Jude 9 KJV: "Yet **Michael the archangel**, when contending with the devil he disputed about the body of Moses, durst not bring against him a railing accusation, but said, The Lord rebuke thee."

This mysterious verse hints at a cosmic-level conflict between Michael and Satan, likely rooted in ancient traditions outside the canonical Old Testament. Some scholars link this to an Aramaic tradition about the Assumption of Moses, but in the Enochian context, it may reflect a much older battle — possibly Michael casting down Lucifer before the Flood, as seen in 1 Enoch 10. Jude could be using the phrase "body of Moses" allegorically or typologically. It may allude to the body of Abel, whose murder by Cain marked the first shedding of innocent blood — possibly placing this dispute in a pre-Sinai, pre-Flood setting.

Book of Jude and 1 Enoch

Jude 1:10 KJV: "But these speak evil of those things which they know not: but what they know naturally, as **brute beasts**, in those things they corrupt themselves."

2 Peter 2:12 KJV: "But these, as **natural brute beasts**, made to be taken and destroyed, speak evil of the things that they understand not; and shall utterly perish in their own corruption;"

Jude 1:10 and 2 Peter 2:12 use nearly identical language to describe false teachers as instinct-driven "brute beasts" who slander what they don't know and perish in their own corruption. 1 Enoch also mentions "beasts of the field" which aligns with Genesis, linking Jude's beast metaphor to pre-flood thought.

Jude 1:11 KJV: "Woe unto them! for they have **gone in the way of Cain** and ran greedily after the error of Balaam for reward and perished in the gainsaying of Core."
This verse explicitly ties Jude's warning back to pre-Flood times with the mention of Cain, the archetype of rebellion, violence, and corrupted sacrifice. "The way of Cain" signals a return to the lawless age of Noah. This matches up with 1 John 3:12,15 and John 8:44 where Jesus compares the Pharisees to Cain.

Jude 1:12 KJV: "These are spots in your feasts of charity, when they feast with you, feeding themselves without fear: clouds they are without water, carried about of winds; trees whose fruit withereth, without fruit, twice dead, plucked up by the roots;" Jude layers metaphors of emptiness and judgment here. "Clouds without water" and "trees without fruit" These false ones blend in ("feasting with you") but are spiritually barren and dead. The phrase "twice dead" may allude to those who were already condemned in the pre-Flood era and are repeating the same path now — a chilling resurrection of the ancient rebellion. Jude 1:4 KJV: "For there are certain men crept in unawares, **who were before of old ordained to this condemnation,** ungodly men, turning the grace of our God into lasciviousness, and denying the only Lord God, and our Lord Jesus

Christ."

Book of Jude and 1 Enoch

Cross-reference:

• Genesis 6:5 KJV– "And God saw that the wickedness of man was great in the earth, and that every imagination of the thoughts of his heart was only evil continually."

• Matthew 24:38 KJV – "For as in the days that were before the flood they were eating and drinking, marrying and giving in marriage, until the day that Noe entered into the ark."

Jesus' words echo Jude's warning: the casual corruption of society, marked by indulgence and spiritual decay, is the sign of imminent judgment — just as in the days of Noah.

Jude 13 KJV: "Raging waves of the sea, foaming out their own shame; **wandering stars**, to whom is reserved the blackness of darkness forever."

This verse ties directly into Aramaic-rooted Enochian cosmology. "Wandering stars" is how 1 Enoch 18:14–16 describes the fallen angels stars that do not obey God's order. They are bound in "a prison for the stars and the host of heaven." Jude is declaring that these modern corrupt individuals are spiritually aligned with the Watchers. The "blackness of darkness" is a direct reference to their cosmic punishment a return to the abyss.

Jude 14-15 KJV: "And **Enoch also, the seventh from Adam**, prophesied of these, saying, Behold, the Lord cometh with ten thousands of his saints, To execute judgment upon all, and to convince all that are ungodly among them of all their ungodly deeds which they have ungodly committed, and of all their hard speeches which ungodly sinners have spoken against him."

Jude explicitly names Enoch as "the seventh from Adam," confirming the patriarchal lineage and connecting back to pre-Flood prophecy. This is a direct quotation from 1 Enoch 1:9, which Jude treats as authoritative prophecy. This isn't a vague endorsement, it's a clear scriptural validation of Enoch's writings.

Jude is not simply quoting Enoch, he is framing all of human corruption and divine judgment through Enoch's lens, warning that the rebellion of the Watchers is repeating in his day and will reach its climax in the last judgment.

Chapter 14
Summary

Summary of Aramaic Roots

This flame isn't a new flame but a old flame that was burning in secret. These are not new teachings but the ancient teachings being reawakened. This is the divine Revelation of Genesis, understanding its long-lost Aramaic Roots.

This is not a doctrine we created, but the interpretation of the scriptures the prophets and apostles knew, the understanding that Christ taught and spoke! The understanding that He died on the cross for! This is not a new religion, but an ancient faith first written down by Enoch, seventh from Adam and great grandfather of Noah.

The words and Blessing of Enoch were banned by the Greco-Roman Church and Canaanite Judaism and continue to be rejected even in the modern era! Christians are taught to read the Hebrew Old Testament from a group that hates our Lord and Savior Jesus Christ. Christians are taught to read the Greek New Testament, that was written by groups that attacked Christians and their teachings.
Why, when from Abraham's time to Christ the language spoken was Aramaic?

The true language of God was rejected, and we were given a Jewish and Gentile account stripping Christianity from its true origin. These same groups reject the book of Enoch, an ancient text passed down from the pre-flood world, matching up with the teachings of Christ!

The Christians that kept the book of Enoch, were attacked in some of the most horrific ways imaginable. This is not by mistake. These big religious groups want the Aramaic Roots erased from human history. They want the world to believe in their version of Christianity. They want you to believe the most powerful religion on earth is nothing more than an off shoot of Judaism.
However, there is Linguistic, Historical, and Biblical evidence pointing towards a root faith developed in Aramaic that existed hundreds of years before Judaism was even thought of! It pre-dates the laws of Moses, the building of the first temple, and the dismantling of the ten tribes of Israel.

Summary of Aramaic Roots

It's foolish to think that Jesus, the King of kings, would need to use the origin story of a religion who hates him to tell us how this all started. The original works of the Old and New Testament are likely Aramaic, with the Hebrew being a later translation. The concepts and teachings were hijacked from Enochian Christianity. This has been hidden by groups like Judaism to have theological dominance over Christians. It has been kept secret by modern Christian groups to prevent the radicalization of western Christianity because they are scared that believers in Christ might start rejecting big church leaders, like the Pope.

Modern historians and occultists mock the Bible and Enoch's words from the Lord by claiming it's pre-dated by occult teachings, when in fact all these ancient faiths are based off the accounts in Genesis and 1 Enoch.

Some chose to go astray from Yeshua and follow the Fallen Angels, like the Sumerian and Canaanite cults. While others changed Enoch's teaching into a more religious earthly practice, like modern Zoroastrianism.

It's truly a modern miracle how some fragments of these ancient Aramaic texts survived to the modern era, resurrecting the scriptures that Christ and the Apostles had, comprehending the inspired sacred knowledge Adam, Enoch, and Noah would have shared before the great flood, and witnessing a divine awakening like never before in the Christian spirit!

Terminology

Aramaic Roots

Aramaic Roots is the restoration of the original teachings passed down from Adam, Enoch, and Noah, preserved in the Aramaic language long before Hebrew or Greek texts. This is the belief system behind Enochian Christianity, stripped of later religious corruption, including Pharisaic Judaism and Roman-influenced Christianity. It focuses on the earliest writings, such as the Book of Enoch, the Targums, and other ancient Aramaic texts that survived through marginalized sects like Essenes and Nazarenes. Aramaic Roots exposes the modern disconnect from these original teachings and returns to the language, worldview, and spiritual truths of the first believers. This is not "Messianic Judaism" or some hybrid theology, it's the unfiltered foundation that came before all of that.

Enochian Christianity

Enochian Christianity is the original belief system that predates Moses, Judaism, and even the birth of Christ, yet it is fully Christian in nature, centered on the worship of the Ancient of Days, obedience to His commandments, and faith in the coming of the Son of Man. It traces its roots to Enoch, the first scribe and prophet, who "walked with God: and he was not; for God took him."
Genesis 5:24 KJV

Though these teachings originate with Adam, Enoch preserved them in written form, making him the foundation of this pre-Mosaic, pre-Judaic Christianity.

This is not a new religion, it is the oldest. The term "Enochian" refers to this ancient, Aramaic-rooted faith, not to the occult garbage of John Dee's so-called "Enochian magic." That 19th-century modern invention is a blasphemous parody. We're reclaiming the term Enochian and restoring it to its rightful place, the holy path laid down by God, through His earliest prophets.

1 Enoch Predicts Its Own Removal

1 Enoch presents itself as divinely inspired scripture, foreseeing both its preservation and corruption, and ultimately its redemption among the righteous in the end times.

"And now, my son Methuselah, all these things I am recounting to thee and writing down for thee! and I have revealed to thee everything, and given thee books concerning all these: so preserve, my son Methuselah, the books from thy father's hand, and (see) that thou deliver them to the generations of the world. Now, therefore, I swear to you, the righteous, by the glory of the Great and Honoured and Mighty One in dominion, and by His greatness I swear to you. I know a mystery, And have read the heavenly tablets, And have seen the holy books, And have found written therein and inscribed regarding them: And now I know this mystery, **that sinners will alter and pervert the words of righteousness in many ways,** and will speak wicked words, and lie, and practice great deceits, and write books concerning their words. But when they write down truthfully all my words in their languages, and do not change or minish ought from my words but write them all down truthfully -all that I first testified concerning them.

Then, I know another mystery,
that books will be given to the righteous and the wise
to become a cause of joy and uprightness and much wisdom.
And to them shall the books be given, and they shall believe in them
and rejoice over them and then shall all the righteous who have learnt
therefrom all the paths of uprightness be recompensed."

The book written by Enoch
"(Enoch indeed wrote this complete doctrine of wisdom,
[which is] praised of all men and a judge of all the earth)
for all my children who dwell on the earth.
And for the future generations who shall observe
uprightness and peace."

1 Enoch 82:1, 1 Enoch 92:1
1 Enoch 103:1-2, 1 Enoch 104:10-11, 1 Enoch 104:12-13

WE ARE THAT FUTURE GENERATION...

Works Cited

- Book of 1 Enoch by R.H. Charles Oxford: The Clarendon Press
- Book of 1 Enoch by Dr. Joseph B. Lumpkin ©2011 All Rights Reserved.
- Australian Journal of Biblical Archeology--online
- Translation Of 1Q Genesis Apocryphon II-XXII - John C. Reeves
- Ephrem The Syrian: Hymns by Kathleen McVey ©1989
- Book of Jubilees by Derek A. Shaver ©2012
- Targum Jonathan--sefaria.org
- The Ages of the World 4Q180-181---moellerhaus.com
- "A Key To The Original Gospels" by George M. Lamas
- Aramaic Word Study--Chaim Bentorah--www.chaimbentorah.com/2021/04/aramaic-word-study-eli-eli-lama-sabachthani/
- Pananion 29--nazarenejudaism.com
- Zohar: Bereshith to Lekh Lekha by Nurho de Manhar [1900-14]--sacred-texts.com
- Tertullian "Apparel of Women" Book 1--newadvent.org
- The Peshitta Holy Bible Translated by Glenn David Bauscher Copyright © 2019
- Chart-Evolution of Religious Teachings created by Brandon Marcin
- Qu'ran--quran.com
- Tafsir--altafsir.com
- Rumi--September 1207–December 1273--13th-century poet
- Targum Job--sefaria.org
- Zarathustra aka Zoroaster 1500-1000 BCE founder of Zoroastrianism
- Book of Tobit--author unknown--bible.usccb.org

Brandon Marcin (MARCIN VIIVIIVII) is an American Christian, Theologian and Social Media Influencer, born in 1994 in Kenosha, Wisconsin and raised in Portland, Oregon. He started studying biblical history and ancient texts in 2012 and in 2020 he began taking his study and content more seriously, amassing millions of views on TikTok.
Also, he is a completely independent recording and performing artist that makes hip-hop and alternative music.

Leona J. Atkinson is an American Christian, Theologian, and Evangelist. She has been a born-again believer in Christ since 1984 when she began deeply studying the bible and doing freelance inspirational writing for many years.
She is the President of SGLY Ministry, founded in 1997.
She graduated from Inste Bible College and received her Certificate of Ministry in 2009.
She is also a 2023 graduate of Christian Leaders Institute.

ANCIENT ARAMAIC ENOCHIAN CHRISTIANITY

יֵשׁוּעַ